THE EVERYTHING®

WEDDING ETIQUETTE BOOK

Revised and Expanded
Second Edition

Insights and advice on handling even the stickiest wedding issues

**Emily Ehrenstein and Laura Morin
with Leah Furman and Elina Furman**

Adams Media Corporation
Holbrook, Massachusetts

Acknowledgments

We'd like to express our deepest gratitude to Janet Anastasio and Michelle Bevilacqua, whose work was the inspiration for this book. Best wishes and thanks to Nancy True and Tami Monahan Forman, who were always there to share their real-life experiences, and to Susan Beale for her topnotch design and production work. Thanks also to the Association of Bridal Consultants, Hazel Bowman of Celebrations by Bowman, and Diane Green of Distinctive Weddings for their expert advice.

Copyright ©2000, Adams Media Corporation. All rights reserved. This book, or parts thereof, may not be reproduced in any form without permission from the publisher; exceptions are made for brief excerpts used in published reviews.

An Everything® Series Book.
Everything® is a registered trademark
of Adams Media Corporation.
www.adamsmedia.com

Published by Adams Media Corporation
260 Center Street, Holbrook, MA 02343

ISBN: 1-58062-454-5

Printed in Canada.

J I H G F E D C B A

Many of the designations used by manufactures and sellers to distinguish their products are claimed as trademarks. Where those designations have appeared in this book and Adams Media was aware of a trademark claim, the designations have been printed in initial capital letters.

Illustrations by Barry Littmann and Kathie Kelleher.

*This book is available at quantity discounts for bulk purchases.
For information, call 1-800-872-5627.*

Contents

Introduction

Are you on the verge of eloping? Do you feel as if you'll scream if one more person tries to give you advice? This is not exactly the way you pictured your blissfully-engaged self. You can still remember the day you said "yes." Oh, the fun you thought you'd have. Planning the wedding, choosing a gown, breaking open the Dom Perignon—talk about the time of your life! Yes, that was a great day, a day when you learned that your dream of being a blushing bride would soon come true. Well, at this point you're probably coming to terms with some of life's harsher realities, and realizing exactly why it's the bride who traditionally does all the blushing. By now, you've probably realized that putting a wedding together can be, well, overwhelming. Not only do you have a hundred different things to worry about, but your mother, future mother-in-law, and just about everyone you know is probably trying to tell you the right and wrong way of doing things. Everyone, it seems, is an expert on wedding etiquette. With so many differing points of view, what's a well-meaning bride to do? Believe it or not, two round-trip tickets to Vegas are not the answer. By following the rules of etiquette, you'll not spend your day in the sun feeling as if you're in the doghouse.

That's where *The Everything® Wedding Etiquette Book* comes in. This book won't tell you where to place the dessert fork, but it will tell you how to solve more contemporary etiquette dilemmas, like how to seat divorced parents at the reception and whether or not your sister can host a wedding shower. It will also tell you how to word wedding invitations, whether or not a cash bar is appropriate, and what to do if a wedding gift arrives damaged.

This book also recognizes that there are no hard and fast rules of etiquette anymore—what's right for one bride may not be right for another. Many questions, especially those dealing with divorced families, have no single correct answer; solutions to these types of dilemmas depend upon the dynamics within your particular family. You should also remember that many questions of etiquette are simply a matter of common sense; others can be avoided altogether through flexibility and communication.

The Everything® Wedding Etiquette Book is designed to relieve some of the stress associated with wedding planning. Within these pages you will find the answers to any type of etiquette dilemma you and your fiancé may face. It will also give you advice and insights on how to plan a fabulous wedding. Keep this book handy, and you'll be prepared for any snags and glitches that may come your way.

Good luck!

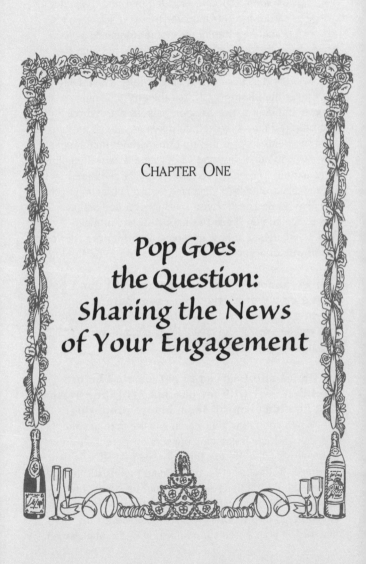

CHAPTER ONE

Pop Goes the Question: Sharing the News of Your Engagement

As soon as you're engaged, the first thing you want to do is tell everyone you see. Don't. If you ever want your mother to speak to you again, resist the temptation. Your families, not Sam the butcher, should be the first to know. And Mom and Dad should be told in person if at all possible. If not, telling them over the phone is OK, but then try to arrange a visit for you and your fiancé as soon as possible. Although getting engaged may very well go down as one of the happiest moments in your life, try to remember that people close to you might respond with a mixed bag of emotions. Your parents can either be thrilled to bits, perturbed by the prospect of losing their daughter, or a combination of the two. The same goes for your best friends and siblings. The way in which you break the happy news can make a great deal of difference in how accepting your intimate relations are of you, your fiancé, and your decision to tie the knot.

Can we announce our engagement if I don't have a ring or we don't have an exact date?

In a word, yes. As soon as he asks you to marry him and you say yes, it's official. Or, as soon as you ask him and he says yes, it's official.

My fiancé and I agreed to get married before talking it over with my parents. Will they be upset that he didn't consult them before proposing?

While you know your parents better than anyone, in this day and age it is highly unusual for parents to frown at a suitor's failure to ask them for their daughter's hand in marriage. In days of yore, the father's permission had to be obtained before an engagement could be struck, but this custom is no longer applicable, as nowadays the decision is clearly up to the bride-to-be (or not-to-be, as the case may be). If your parents are informed of the engagement promptly after the proposal, there should be no hard feelings whatsoever.

How do we decide which set of parents to tell first?

Since it's unlikely that both sets of parents live in the same city or state as the bride and groom, distance usually plays a part in determining which set of parents hears the news first. However, the bride-to-be's family is traditionally told first, with the groom's family being told soon after. After everyone is told, the groom's family usually contacts your parents, either through a short note or phone call. If your parents are divorced, his parents should call the parent who raised you, and then call the other parent later if the two of you are still close. If the two families live close by, they can have brunch or drinks together, and each can get an idea of the other's expectations for the wedding. This gathering can take place with or without you and your fiancé. And if weeks go by and your beloved's parents haven't made the initial contact, your parents can call them, or you and your fiancé can try to arrange a meeting.

What if my parents and fiancé have never met?

Try to bring your future hubby home to spend a few days with your family before sharing the news. Don't just walk in and say "Hi, everybody. Meet your future son-in-law!" Let your parents and fiancé get to know each other before announcing your engagement.

I'm not sure how my parents will react . . . any suggestions?

Tell them in person—alone. If you suspect that your parents will be less than thrilled about your choice of a husband, you don't want your honey there to see the look of disappointment in your father's eyes. Telling Mom and Dad without your fiancé present enables everyone to speak with candor.

Can I wear a family heirloom as my engagement ring?

Of course! Wearing a family heirloom is a wonderful way to preserve the memory of a beloved family member. And you should feel honored if your fiancé wants you to wear an heirloom from his side of the family. If you both decide to go with an heirloom instead of a new ring, your fiancé may decide to reset the stones into a different ring or buy you another piece of jewelry, like a tennis bracelet or necklace, instead.

"Mom"? "Dad"? How about "Hey You"?

At some point in your engagement, the question of what to call your fiancé's parents is bound to come up. This is one of those issues that, on paper, shouldn't be that difficult, but always manages to cause some degree of awkwardness or tension between your families. Many couples look forward to having children so that they can get rid of this issue and just call everyone Grandma and Grandpa. Believe it or not, many people choose to avoid the matter altogether by not calling their in-laws anything at all. Needless to say, choosing this mode of conduct only compounds the problem as days turn into months and you're still stuck dreading the prospect of talking to your well-meaning mother-in-law for something as trivial as lack of a proper address.

How do I find out what my in-laws want me to call them?

Most likely they will say something directly either to you or your fiancé. If not, have your fiancé find out for you. In many cases, engaged couples just continue to call the in-laws whatever they did before their engagement (Mr. and Mrs. Brown, John and Sylvia, etc.)

Popping the Question

Short of a coin toss, there are less traditional ways of asking for someone's hand in marriage than getting down on bended knee and begging. Don't worry if your fiancé didn't go exactly by the book; when it comes to asking for a hand in marriage, almost anything goes. In fact, the last few years have seen media outlets reporting some lovers popping the question as imaginatively as possible, using such devices as:

- Airplane banner
- Billboard
- Movie theater trailer
- TV talk show
- Halftime announcement at a football game
- Message on the giant screen of a baseball game
- Live balloon delivery
- Custom fortune cookie
- Singing waiters
- Request line on rock radio
- Groom disguised as clown in circus

What if they want me to call them something I'm not comfortable with?

If they want you to call them "Mom" and "Dad" for instance, explain to them that you don't feel comfortable calling anyone but your own parents "Mom" and "Dad." Suggest calling them whatever your fiancé is calling your parents, instead.

What should I call my fiancé's stepparents?

The best and easiest solution is to call them whatever your fiancé does.

Now that we're engaged, do I have to refer to my boyfriend as "my fiancé"?

Yes. The designation of "boyfriend" and "girlfriend" is no longer sufficient. Once you two decide to get married, and until such time as you do, you should refer to each other as "my fiancé." That is, unless you have a better idea, such as "my intended" or, better yet, "my betrothed."

Whatever Happened to the Nuclear Family?

As many of us know, life would be a lot easier if we were living in a different era, namely a time when stepmothers were known only to Cinderella and the Cleavers ruled the TV. Divorced parents, ex-spouses and children from previous marriages can all bring some tension to what is supposed to be the happiest event in your life. In all of these cases, a little tact and thoughtfulness can go a long way.

My parents are divorced. Whom should I tell first?

This is probably one area where the etiquette police can't get you. You know your family better than anyone does. Do what you feel most comfortable with.

What if one of us has children?

If one of you has children, tell them right away. Don't risk letting them feel excluded. They will want to know how a new mommy or daddy will affect them. While it is not essential that children of a divorce give their consent (and it isn't likely that they will at first), tremendous compassion should be used in breaking the news, for they will probably regard it as a repudiation of their other parent.

How should I let my ex-spouse know I'm getting remarried?

If you have children together, your ex-spouse shouldn't find out through the grapevine. A phone call would be fine, but be prepared for questions about alimony payments or custody arrangements. If you don't have kids, then whether or not you tell your ex-spouse depends on your relationship with him or her.

Stop the Presses: We're Getting Married!

After you've told your assorted parents, stepparents, grandparents, and ex-spouses, the time has come for you to share your joy with your friends and coworkers. This can be done pretty easily; as soon as someone sees that ring on your finger, the news will spread like wildfire. Once again, we caution you to use great care when disclosing the news to your nearest and dearest of pals. While it's OK to let the ring speak for itself with casual friends and acquaintances, special friends deserve special attention. Depending on how close you are, these intimates should be enlightened either in person or over the phone as soon as you're done telling your parents and assorted relatives.

Should we announce our engagement in the newspaper?

Once you've told close friends and relatives, you may choose to put formal announcements in the newspapers in your hometown and the city in which you work. The information is pretty standard: names and occupations of the bride, groom, and their parents, and schools attended. Some papers have a standard form you need to fill out; check with your local paper for specifications. Usually, a photograph of the bride-to-be (but not the groom) may also be sent.

Are the bride's parents the only ones who can make the engagement announcement? What if my parents are divorced?

The protocol for who makes the engagement announcement is as follows: Normally, the parents of the bride-to-be make the announcement of their daughter's engagement. If the parents are divorced, then the mother makes the announcement, but the father must be mentioned. If both parents are deceased, then a close relative does the honors. If the couple are older and have been on their own, they may make the announcement themselves.

Does our engagement need to be a particular length of time?

That depends. If you want to plan a wedding that will dwarf Princess Di's, you'd better leave yourself at least a year. Generally, engagements last from 3 to eighteen 18, but remember that the more time you give yourself to plan, the more time you'll have to revise your plan if things don't go smoothly.

Let the Parties Begin!

Once all the major players have been notified, tradition indicates that someone, usually your parents, will throw a party in honor of you and your fiancé. This party can be as formal or informal as the hosts would like. Aside from celebrating the engagement, the point is to give you and your fiancé an official coming out party, a sort of couple's debut into society. If you have not yet met all of each other's friends, this party will give you two the opportunity to mingle and get the old gang accustomed to the new situation. The families will also have a chance to bond with their newfound in-laws as well as get better acquainted with the other people in both of your lives. The engagement party marks the official beginning of party season, and from this point forward, you'd better get used to being the center of attention.

When is the engagement party held?

The engagement party should be held before your announcement appears in the newspapers, or soon after. If you're planning on a short engagement, the party should be held as soon as possible so as not to interfere with any bridal showers or bachelorette parties. You and your fiancé can also decide to throw a party for yourselves, and then surprise guests with your news.

What is the most traditional way to have an engagement party?

The parents or mother of the bride host a party at which the formal announcement is made and the groom is presented to the friends and family (who may already

Newspaper Engagement Announcement Worksheet

To make the wedding announcement as easy as possible, use the following fill-in-the-blank worksheet and check it off your list in minutes.

To appear in _(name of newspaper)_ newspaper on _(date)_

Names of the bride's parents:

Address:

_____

_____

_____

_____

Telephone number with area code:

_____

Mr. and Mrs. _(bride's parents' names)_ of _(their city, if out of town)_ announce the engagement of their daughter, _(bride's first and middle name)_, to _(groom's first and last name)_, the son of Mr. and Mrs. _(groom's parents' names)_, of _(groom's parents' city)_. A _(month/season)_ wedding is planned. (Or, No date has been set for the wedding.)

know him anyway, or should by now). That is where the mother makes the announcement. The announcement is supposed to be a surprise, so no mention of it is made on the party invitation. If the bride lives in a different city from her parents, the party may be held in her city so that more of her friends can be in attendance.

Can we have more than one engagement party?

Of course. The bride's parents usually have first dibs on throwing the engagement party, but the groom's parents may also want to celebrate with their families and friends.

Should I expect gifts at an engagement party?

Gifts aren't required, but just in case, you may want to begin spreading word of where you've registered. And of course, you should promptly send written thank-you notes for any gifts you receive.

Do I have to register? Can't I just let people bring whatever they want?

By no means is joining a bridal registry a prerequisite for marriage. However, you should keep in mind that this is a service that can only help you and your guests. It will keep your invitees free from the frustration of trying to please the couple that seems to have it all, and decrease your chances of winding up with enough food processors to start a successful smoothie venture. Better department and specialty stores offer a free bridal registry service and a staff consultant who will advise the bride and groom on what items they might need to start a home. The registry keeps a list, advises inquirers about what's on it and how much it costs, and keeps the bride posted on progress.

What is a trousseau?

The idea of a registry is to provide the bride with a trousseau, or the things that she and her husband will probably need during their first year. The word trousseau is a throwback to a time when brides brought their own "things" with them into their new home: doilies, fine linens, lingerie, and other such personal items. The small bundle of stuff was called a trousseau. In time, the standard dowry eclipsed what one could carry in a small bundle, but the name stuck just the same.

The days of exquisite homemade needlepoint and lace may be passed, but the need for a new bride to begin her marriage with a "hope chest" has not. Although in olden times the bride and her mother were responsible for filling the hope chest, modernity has spread the duty to include family and friends. The point of the exercise is to help the couple start building a home. The trousseau includes:

Bed linen (at least three sets for the master bedroom and two for the guest room)

- ❑ Fitted sheets
- ❑ Flat sheets
- ❑ Pillowcases
- ❑ Pillows
- ❑ Blankets
- ❑ Mattress pad or cover
- ❑ Bedspread or comforter

Table linen

- ❑ Napkins for eight
- ❑ Large formal tablecloth
- ❑ Napkins and plastic mats for informal use
- ❑ Cotton or pad liner for tablecloth
- ❑ Smaller tablecloths and napkins for "children's table"

Bath linen

- ☐ Four large bath towels
- ☐ Matching hand towels
- ☐ Matching face cloths
- ☐ Midsize "hair towels" for women's hair
- ☐ Bath mat
- ☐ Shower curtain
- ☐ Small guest towels

Cookware

- ☐ Frying pan
- ☐ Covered saucepans (large and small)
- ☐ Tea kettle
- ☐ Utensil set
- ☐ Baking pans

China (formal service for eight, sometimes twelve, plus everyday service for eight)

- ☐ Dinner plates
- ☐ Salad plates
- ☐ Cups and saucers
- ☐ Creamer and sugar bowl
- ☐ Salt and pepper shakers
- ☐ Soup bowls
- ☐ Bread and butter plates
- ☐ Serving platters
- ☐ Glassware/crystal
- ☐ Water goblets
- ☐ Wine glasses
- ☐ Cocktail glasses
- ☐ Champagne glasses

Silverware (formal service for eight, sometimes twelve, plus everyday service for eight)

- ❏ Knives
- ❏ Dinner forks
- ❏ Salad forks
- ❏ Soup spoons
- ❏ Teaspoons

Silverware (additions to formal service)

- ❏ Butter knife
- ❏ Fish knife
- ❏ Dessert fork
- ❏ Shrimp fork
- ❏ Iced tea spoon
- ❏ Steak knife
- ❏ Specialized serving utensils (carving knife, slotted spoon, pie server, gravy boat and spoon, chafing dish)

Any bridal registry will be only too happy to provide an exhaustive list of gift items. The understanding in assembling a trousseau is that couples just starting out their lives together may not need to do formal entertaining and that everyday service will do for the first year or at least until they become more established.

I am afraid that some of my guests won't be able to afford the items on my registry. Can I open another registry at a less expensive store?

If your guests hail from a wide range of incomes, registering at two or more stores (upscale, moderate, utilitarian, etc.) is not only appropriate but encouraged.

Beyond the Trousseau

While sheets, napkins, and towels are important, new-lyweds cannot live by linen alone. The following are some wedding gifts that have proved popular and well received in recent years. Any of the following items can be added to your bridal registry.

- Videocassette recorder
- Camcorder
- Laser disc player
- Microwave oven
- Food processor
- CD-ROM drive for computer
- Fine cutlery
- High-end cookware
- Place settings (china, silver, crystal)
- Garage door opener
- Computer software
- Closet storage/shelving
- Carpeting (gift certificate), or fine rugs
- Floor or table lamp
- Clock radio
- Coffeemaker

A Piece of the Rock

I don't want to spend too much on my engage-ment ring, but neither do I want a substandard diamond. How do I go about making sure that I get a good deal without appearing as if the ring is the most important part of the engagement?

A great deal of effort goes into the quest for an engagement ring. Your best bet is to discuss the matter openly with your fiancé. Explain how important it is that you find a good ring, since the only time you'll be taking it off is when you wash your hair, if that. Talk about your financial concerns and decide on a budget from the get go. Involve your fiancé in every step of the engagement ring hunt, no doubt he'll quickly realize that your emphasis on this major purchase is well warranted.

How much should an engagement ring cost?

While there's always the big talk about making two months' salary last forever, there are no hard and fast rules in this department—perhaps the one general rule that no engagement ring should cost more than you and your future spouse can afford to spend. Of course, a good quality ring will almost invariably set you back a few thousand dollars, at the very least. Still, the price of the ring should be proportional to the size of your income. Upwardly mobile couples often settle on modest engagement rings, substantially upgrading the stone at such time as their ship comes in.

My fiancé gave me a family heirloom as an engagement ring. The problem is that it has an emerald stone. All I've ever seen are diamond engagement rings; is an emerald ring OK?

Unconventional and improper are not one and the same. Although diamonds are the most popular choice for engagement rings, they are by no means the only acceptable alternative. In fact, the custom of presenting a diamond engagement ring actually stems from medieval Italy, where precious stones (read: diamonds, rubies, emeralds, sapphires) were seen as part of the groom's payment for the bride. The gift of such stones symbolized the groom's intent to marry. So, in answer to your question, giving antique rings that have been worn by generations past is a wonderful tradition that can connect you to your new family much more effectively than any store-bought ring, diamond or otherwise.

My fiancé has been married before. Is it appropriate for me to wear his former wife's wedding ring?

Absolutely not. If either you or your fiancé has previously been married, don't use the rings from that marriage in your new one. Wearing the rings that were part of a marriage to someone else is insensitive and in very poor taste. What do you do with those old rings? Some choose to sell them to make a complete break with the past, but there are other options. Women may have their engagement ring reset and worn as regular jewelry. If there are children from the previous marriage, you may decide to put the rings aside for them.

Birthstones by Month

January:	Garnet
February:	Amethyst
March:	Aquamarine
April:	Diamond
May:	Emerald
June:	Pearl
July:	Ruby
August:	Peridot
September:	Sapphire
October:	Opal
November:	Topaz
December:	Turquoise

**I'm perfectly happy with the engage-
ment ring that my fiancé gave me,
but I was wondering whether it's
appropriate for me to wear it as a
wedding ring after we get married?
Is it absolutely necessary to have
two rings?**

Certainly not, to the second question
that is. Wearing your engagement ring as a wedding ring is
a very viable option for today's brides. Although many
brides who opt for one ring choose not to wear it until the
wedding ceremony, wearing the ring while you're engaged
is well within the bounds of etiquette. Just make sure that
you take off the wedding ring and get it to the ring
bearer/best man come wedding day.

Do our wedding bands have to match exactly?

Although many couples today wear matching wedding
bands, there is absolutely no rule to this effect. While
men's wedding rings are traditionally unadorned, women's
can be more elaborate, so go ahead and choose a band
that suits your taste. Oftentimes, brides who went without
an engagement ring choose to buy a diamond wedding
band, while the groom sticks with a plain band. Many couples also choose to engrave the inside of their bands with
their initials and the date of their wedding.

Who traditionally pays for the
wedding bands?

The laws of etiquette have it that you pay for your
fiancé's wedding band while he pays for yours. Of course,
no one would be offended if you two decided to go a different route.

Know the Four Cs

If you decide on a diamond engagement ring, pay attention to the four marks of diamond quality when you're shopping around. The stone you purchase should pass the test in each of these categories:

1. **Clarity:** Clarity is the most important factor in determining the beauty of a given stone: a stone with low clarity, for example, will have a number of imperfections when viewed under a gemologist's magnifying glass.

2. **Cut:** The cut of a diamond is the stone's physical configuration, the result of the process whereby the rough gem is shaped. Common shapes include the "round" (or "brilliant"), pearl shaped, oval, and marquise cuts.

3. **Color:** The color of the diamond is also a major factor in determining its value. Stones that are colorless are considered to be perfect. The object, then, is to find a stone that is as close to colorless as possible.

4. **Carat:** The carat weight refers to the actual size of the stone.

What's It All Mean?

The Ring Finger –
The third finger on the left hand is considered the ring finger. All engagement and wedding rings are worn there because centuries ago that finger was believed to be connected by a vein directly to the heart.

The Wedding Ring –
The idea of the wedding ring itself dates back to ancient times, when a caveman husband would wrap circles of braided grass around his bride's wrists and ankles, believing it would keep her spirit from leaving her body. The bands evolved into leather, carved stone, metal, and later silver and gold. (Luckily, you only have to wear them on your finger nowadays—and the groom usually reciprocates.)

Once we're married, do we have to wear the wedding rings at all times?

Although married people are generally expected to become one with their wedding bands, with the husband and wife both wearing their bands on the same fingers, there are times when you are allowed to temporarily part with your ring. These include athletics, chores, radiology, and the like. Mind you, girls'- or guys'-night-out does not fall under the heading of "good time to remove wedding band."

Jewelry Shopping Tips

Your first step in the search for a ring should
be to consult with a reputable jeweler. Referrals from
experienced family and friends are the best way to find
someone trustworthy. Should your social circle not yield
many results, pick a store that appeals to you, stocks
jewelry in your price range, and is a member of the
American Gem Society. While members of the AGS
must meet high standards of quality and reputability,
you should still avoid taking any chances by . . .

- Shopping around. Even if you fall head over heels
  in love with the first ring you set eyes on, a little
  perspective never hurt anyone. Comparing selections from other jewelers should give you a better
  idea of fair pricing as well as your options.
- Negotiating. Don't hesitate to ask if the price is
  negotiable. Like car salespeople, jewelry salespeople expect to do their fair share of haggling.
- Making the final sale contingent upon your taking
  the ring to an appraiser of your choice to verify
  value and price. There are unscrupulous jewelers
  who will try to dupe you into buying a ring for
  much more than it's worth by having their
  appraiser (or one they recommend) "confirm" the
  ring's inflated value.
- Getting a purchase agreement that includes stipulations for sizing and potential return. Does the
  store offer a money-back guarantee if the ring is
  returned within the designated time frame?
- Getting a written appraisal and insurance. It's not
  romantic, but insurance purposes demand that
  you get a written appraisal that describes the ring
  and cites its value. Insure your ring under your
  homeowner's or renter's policy.

CHAPTER TWO

Money, Money: The Budget

Some couples have been known to spend upwards of $1 million on their wedding receptions. Others have been able to bring their costs down to the $100,000 mark. Most, however, have managed to come up with creative ways to keep the expense to a minimum while ensuring that a good time is had by all. Guess which group must contend with the most budget-induced headaches? Unless you're one of the lucky ones, money will be the biggest problem of your wedding. The questions of how much to spend and who gets to spend it can quickly become overwhelming. No single issue in wedding planning causes more heartburn than the question of who pays for what. While tradition dictates that the bride's family bears the brunt of financial responsibility for the wedding and reception, today, the groom's parents often offer to pay for portions of the reception (liquor or music, for instance), or the bride and groom may finance all or part of the wedding themselves.

When money is an object, which it almost always is, and quality is of the essence, tradition may have to go the way of the curtsy. As long as all parties handle the financial dealings with care, there is no reason why you can't work out the details to everyone's satisfaction.

What is the traditional breakdown of expenses?
The bride and her family usually pay for:
- 🕊 the bride's dress and accessories
- 🕊 invitations, reception cards, and announcements
- 🕊 the fee for the ceremony site

- the flowers for the ceremony and reception
- the attendants' bouquets
- the bride's father's and grandfather's boutonnières
- music for the ceremony and reception
- the groom's wedding ring and gift
- photography
- housing and gifts for the bridesmaids
- limousines or other rented cars
- all reception costs, including site rental, food, liquor, and decorations.

The groom and his family traditionally pay for:

- the bride's wedding and engagement rings
- the bride's bouquet and gift
- the marriage license
- the officiant's fee
- corsages for the mothers and grandmothers
- boutonnières for the groom, his wedding party, his father, and grandfathers
- the ushers' housing and gifts
- the rehearsal dinner
- the honeymoon

The bride's attendants pay for:

- their dresses and accessories
- a shower gift
- part of the bridal shower and bachelorette party
- transportation to and from the wedding
- a gift for the couple

The groom's attendants should pay for:

- their tuxedoes or suits
- the bachelor party
- transportation to and from the wedding
- a gift for the couple

My parents aren't well-off. Can I ask my fiancé's parents to pay for part of the wedding?

Try to keep your wedding on a scale that is within your family's budget. But if you or your fiancé want something more elaborate than your parents can realistically afford, or if you think his parents will want a big wedding, don't ask them to contribute money. That might lead to some awkward moments between you and his family. Your fiancé, not you, should talk to his parents about a possible contribution to your wedding.

My parents are paying for the wedding. Does that mean I don't get a say in the planning?

No matter who's paying for the wedding, you and your fiancé are the only people who should decide what your wedding will be like. While you should respect your parents' wishes and concerns, you should retain ultimate control over the wedding. If your parents refuse to give up the reins, you and your fiancé may want to consider picking up more of the expenses yourselves.

If we're on a limited budget, can we have a cash bar at the reception?

While cash bars have traditionally been considered taboo at receptions, they are steadily becoming more commonplace. Many couples are choosing to eliminate the open bar because of either budgetary restrictions or concern for their guests' safety. If you're worried that a free-flowing supply of alcohol will drain your budget or encourage your guests to drink and drive, you have several alternatives. You can offer a limited open bar before dinner and then switch to champagne or wine for dinner. Or you could offer wine service during the cocktail hour, table wine during dinner, and a champagne toast. If you still feel that some guests won't be happy unless hard liquor is provided, you can offer a cash bar for all or part of the reception.

My parents are paying for the reception. If my fiancé's parents want to invite a lot more people than mine, shouldn't they offer to cover the extra cost?

The families of the bride and groom should try to have a balanced guest list. But if your future father-in-law insists on inviting all of his great-aunts and second and third cousins, your fiancé should speak with his parents about contributing some money to defray costs.

We're on a limited budget. Can we use the ceremony flowers at the reception, too?

Of course! Using the same flowers at both sites is a great way to save money. Simply ask one or two reliable friends to be in charge of transporting the flowers to the reception right after the ceremony. Make sure these friends have a big car and a flair for decoration; you don't want to walk into the reception hall and see a pile of flowers sitting in the middle of the dance floor.

I just found out that my church is playing host to another wedding ceremony on the same day as mine. Would it be OK for me to ask whether the other couple wants to use the same flowers and split the cost?

Certainly. If the other couple is willing, you'll save a bundle. Of course, you won't be able to reuse these flowers at your reception, but if that was never your plan to begin with, then it's a win-win proposition. If, however, the other couple declines, accept their wishes graciously and look for another way to cut costs.

Our reception site prohibits the throwing of rice, birdseed, etc. How can we let guests know of this?

The tradition of throwing rice began in Asia. Rice (which symbolizes fertility) was thrown at the couple in the hope that this would bring a marriage yielding many children.

Because this practice can be so messy, many reception sites, churches, and synagogues prohibit the throwing of rice or birdseed on their property. If this is true of your site, be sure to let your attendants know; they are usually the ones who provide guests with the rice or birdseed. *Note:* Those considering using rice in their ceremony might choose to use birdseed as it gives off the same theatrical effect but is not deadly to the nearby birds like rice is. The bird's digestive system cannot handle any amount of rice, which expands in their stomachs and kills them.

My fiancé and I are on a tight budget. Is it necessary to give favors to guests?

Favors aren't required, but most couples choose to give their guests a small gift as a memento of their wedding. These can be as simple or elaborate as you'd like, depending upon your budget. If you're having a theme wedding, it's nice to have a memento to correspond with your theme. Other ideas for favors include: small boxes of chocolate or candy-coated almonds, packets of seeds, or decorative figurines. Be creative!

To Tip or Not to Tip?

Even the most budget-conscious brides and grooms often overlook one very substantial expense—tips! Depending upon the size of your reception, tipping can easily add from a few hundred to a few thousand extra dollars to your costs. Many wedding professionals even include a gratuity in their contract, and then expect an additional tip at the reception. As a result, who to tip and how much to tip can often be perplexing dilemmas. Although tipping is, for the most part, expected, it is never required— it's simply an extra reward for extraordinary service. Exactly how much or whom you tip is completely at your discretion. The following are simply guidelines, not rules:

- ✿ Caterers and reception site managers usually have gratuities of 15–20 percent included in their contracts. These are usually paid in advance by the host of the reception. If the caterer or manager has been exceptionally helpful, you may wish to give him or her an additional tip, usually $1–$2 per guest.
- ✿ Wait staff usually receive 15–20 percent of the food bill. Caterers sometimes include this gratuity in their contract. But if the tip is not included, give the tip to the head waiter or maitre d' during the reception.
- ✿ Bartenders should be tipped 15–20 percent of the total bar bill. If their gratuity is already included in the catering contract, an additional 10 percent tip should be paid by the host during the reception. Don't allow the bartender to accept tips from guests; ask him to put up a small sign that says "Please, no tipping."
- ✿ Restroom, coat check, or parking attendants should be prepaid by the host, usually $1–$2 per guest or car. Ask the staff not to accept tips from guests.

- Limousine drivers usually receive 15–20 percent of the bill. Any additional tips are at the host's discretion.
- Musicians or DJs may be tipped if their performance was exceptional. Tips usually run about $25 per band member. DJs are tipped about 15–20 percent of their fee.
- Florists, photographers, and bakers are not usually tipped; you simply pay a flat fee for their services.
- An officiant is never tipped; he or she receives a flat fee for performing the service. A religious officiant may ask for a small donation, around $20, for his or her house of worship, but a civil officiant is not allowed to accept tips.

CHAPTER THREE

The Few, the Proud, the Soon-to-Be-Broke: Your Wedding Party

O nce the initial euphoria of your engagement wears off, once that ring stops feeling strange on your finger, once you begin to realize that you're not just getting married, you're planning an event, the time has come for you and your future hubby to choose the wedding party. Depending upon how many siblings and good friends you and your fiancé have, this can be either a very easy or a very difficult task. You need people you can lean on for support. People who have been there for you through thick and through thin. People who would not only refrain from whining about donning the lavender chiffon dress you so meticulously picked out, but who would gladly pay for the privilege. In other words, you'll need people who owe you—big time.

How many attendants should I have?

The number of bridesmaids/ushers you and your fiancé have is up to you, but in general, the more formal the wedding, the more bridesmaids you have. A good rule of thumb is to have at least one usher for every 50 guests, and then a corresponding number of bridesmaids. Of course, you can always have more attendants if you desire.

Do I need to have the same number of bridesmaids and ushers?

You shouldn't ask the cousin you can't stand to be in your wedding just because your fiancé has chosen one more attendant than you. Besides, it can't hurt to have an extra usher or two. If you're worried about symmetry in the processional or recessional, two ushers can always escort one bridesmaid or the bridesmaids can walk out alone. As for the scheduled dances at the reception, you can either have one of the "extras" dance with their date or another special guest or just skip the dancing altogether. If you have a couple of extra ushers, don't worry about it; they probably won't mind not dancing.

Are married/pregnant bridesmaids appropriate?

There's nothing wrong with having married attendants. They're still called bridesmaids, but a married maid of honor is called a matron of honor. For pregnant attendants, many designers now offer maternity-style bridesmaid dresses. Bear in mind that if your matron of honor will be eight and a half months pregnant at the time of your wedding, you may need a standby.

Can I have attendants of different sexes?

If your best friend is a guy, there's no reason why he shouldn't be included in your wedding party. Just don't make him wear a dress, dance with an usher, or do any of the traditionally "feminine" duties, such as helping you get into your wedding gown or arranging your train and veil. If he's taking the place of your maid of honor, he's called the honor attendant; if not, he's simply another attendant. He stands on your side, and in the processional and recessional, he can walk in before the rest of the bride's attendants, or, if there are more bridesmaids than ushers, escort one of the bridesmaids. Also, it's perfectly acceptable for your fiancé to have a female usher. She's still called an usher, but she shouldn't escort female guests to their seats.

I have two best friends, and I can't choose between them without risking hurt feelings. Can I have two maids of honor?

Fortunately, it is no impropriety in having two honor attendants. In fact, choosing two maids/matrons of honor, or a maid and matron of honor as the case may be, should prove beneficial to both honor attendants, as it will lighten their load of responsibility. Instead of asking one friend to plan the shower and the bachelorette party, as well to help with the ceremony and the invitations, the duties could be split right down the middle. As long as you inform both honor attendants of their co-MOH status, and help guide them through the task of divvying up responsibilities, you will likely find that two maids are better than one.

Wow, I Never Knew I Was So Popular

Choosing a set number of bridesmaids from your many friends and family members can often be quite difficult. And adding his family to the mix can make it worse. Brides often feel obligated to have certain people in their wedding even if they're not that close. So don't bow to your mother's pressure to have your cousin as a bridesmaid if you really don't like her.

Do I have to include immediate family before friends?

No. Bridesmaids are supposed to be the people closest to you, so if you haven't talked to your sister since she moved across the country three years ago, there's no rule that states you must have her as a bridesmaid. The same goes for your fiancé's sister. However, not asking them may cause family strife, so think twice before excluding them from your wedding party.

What are some other ways to involve friends in the ceremony?

If you're afraid that 15 bridesmaids and 10 ushers might look a bit pretentious, you can always find something else for friends to do at the wedding. They could read a poem or passage from Scripture during the ceremony, take charge of the guest book, or hand out programs. If they have a good singing voice or can play an instrument, ask them to perform your favorite song. In Jewish ceremonies, holding the chuppah, or marriage canopy, is a position of honor.

And according to California law, anyone can become an officiant for a day, so those of you tying the knot in the Golden State can ask a friend to perform the ceremony.

What are the age guidelines for flower girls/junior bridesmaids?

If you or your fiancé have younger relatives, you might want to let them play a part in your ceremony. This is especially true if one of you has a child from a previous marriage. Junior bridesmaids are usually between 10 and 14, while flower girls are younger. Little boys, usually under 10, can be ringbearers. Other little boys and girls, called trainbearers, can walk behind the bride, carrying her train. Try to avoid having children under five in your wedding; their behavior can be pretty unpredictable. And if you just have too many nieces/nephews from which to choose, you might want to forget about having kids in the ceremony altogether. Hell hath no fury like a mother scorned.

Do I have to have a flower girl and a ringbearer? What exactly are their responsibilities?

Etiquette does not dictate that you should have either at your wedding. These roles are there for the purpose of incorporating children in your ceremony. Also, let's not forget that flower girls and ringbearers can look very cute and add some style to your procession. In general, its young family members who are chosen as flower girl or ring bearer (the distinction is no longer gender-specific). The flower child walks down the aisle ahead of the bride and scatters flower petals at her feet. The ring-bearer carries a velvet cushion or silver tray on which the wedding bands are held until needed. Both duties earn "oohs" and "aahs" from the guests.

My older sister is my matron of honor, but I also want to include my 12 year-old sister as an honor attendant. How would I go about doing this?

Recognizing your younger sister is a great idea. Girls of junior bridesmaid age who are given an honor position are called maidens of honor. While you can't count on your younger sister to plan the wedding shower and the bachelorette party, including her along with your older sister should make her feel included and an active participant in the wedding.

My fiancé wants to have ushers in addition to groomsmen. I thought these were one and the same. Who's right?

You both are. Usually, the groomsmen carry out all the ushers' responsibilities (in terms of seating guests) and are often simply called ushers as a result. However, it is entirely appropriate for your fiancé to give the seating duties to his other friends, thereby enabling even more people to feel like an important part of the wedding ceremony.

Attendants' Duties

Once the future bride anoints her chosen ones, life is supposed to get easier for her, right? Well, ideally, yes. But oftentimes, the bridesmaids and ushers aren't sure what

The Mother of the Bride

Though you may not realize it, the mother of the bride is considered to be part of the wedding party. After all, your father gets his moment in the sun when he walks you down the aisle—why not the woman who gave you life? At the beginning of the ceremony, the mother is the last person seated before the processional begins. But, like your attendants, she has plenty to do before the wedding, including:

- ❦ Helping the bride in choosing her gown and accessories and in assembling a trousseau
- ❦ Helping the bride select bridesmaids' attire
- ❦ Coordinating her own attire with the mother of the groom
- ❦ Working with the bride and the groom's family to assemble a guest list and seating plan
- ❦ Helping address and mail invitations
- ❦ Helping the attendants coordinate the bridal shower
- ❦ Assisting the bride in any of the hundreds of things she may need help with before the ceremony
- ❦ Occupying a place of honor at the ceremony
- ❦ Standing at the beginning of the receiving line
- ❦ In most instances, acting as hostess of the reception
- ❦ Occupying a seat of honor at the parents' table

they're supposed to do before or at the wedding. It used to be that bridesmaids' main functions were to guard the bride from evil spirits and bear witness that she was not being forced into marriage against her will. Meanwhile, the best man was charged with the task of keeping potential abductors from absconding with the bride prior to the wedding day. But that was then, and this is now. In general, members of the wedding party are supposed to pay for their own clothes and transportation, attend all prewedding parties for the couple, and provide moral support for the bride and groom.

The Maid/Matron of Honor

The maid of honor (or, if married, matron of honor) is the bride's legal witness and personal assistant throughout the wedding process. She exists, foremost, to help the bride.

It is she who precedes the bride down the aisle, holds the groom's ring (in a double-ring ceremony), and adjusts the bride's train. In the receiving line she stands at the groom's left and later sits to his left at the reception. Afterward, she helps the bride change into getaway clothes. She may also host the wedding shower and collect money from the other bridesmaids to choose their gift to the bride.

- Helps the bride with addressing envelopes, recording wedding gifts, shopping, and other pre-wedding tasks
- Arranges a bridal shower
- Helps the bride arrange her train and veil at the altar
- Brings the groom's ring to the ceremony site

- 🐾 Holds the bride's bouquet while she exchanges rings with the groom
- 🐾 Signs the wedding certificate
- 🐾 Stands in the receiving line (optional)
- 🐾 Holds the groom's wedding ring
- 🐾 Makes sure the bride looks perfect for all the pictures
- 🐾 Dances with the best man during the attendants' dance at the reception
- 🐾 Participates in the bouquet toss if single

The Bridesmaids

- 🐾 Help the bride get dressed and ready on the wedding day
- 🐾 Participate in the bouquet toss if single
- 🐾 Help organize and run the bridal shower
- 🐾 Assist the bride and maid of honor with prewedding errands or tasks
- 🐾 Stand in receiving line (optional)

The Best Man

As the groom's legal witness, the best man should help the groom any way possible. Where the bride has her entire family to support her, it is the best man who looks out for his friend, the groom.

Big brothers and close friends are usually chosen as best men, although this can vary depending on age and experience. The best man's foremost job is to get the groom to his wedding on time, and, ahem, sober.

At the reception the best man mingles. He is not part of the receiving line.

- Organizes the bachelor party
- Drives the groom to the ceremony
- Brings the bride's ring to the ceremony site
- Gives the officiant his fee immediately before or after the ceremony (provided by the groom's family)
- Gives other service providers such as the chauffeur, their fees (optional)
- Returns the groom's attire (if rented)
- Oversees the transfer of gifts to a secure location after the reception
- Helps the groom get ready and arrive on time for every wedding-related function
- Holds the bride's ring during the ceremony
- Signs the marriage license as a witness
- Escorts the maid of honor in the recessional
- Sits for pictures with the wedding party and the groom
- Dances with the maid of honor during the attendants' dance at the reception
- Usually sits to the right of the bride at the head table
- Gives the first toast at the reception
- May drive the couple to the reception and/or the hotel if there is no hired driver
- Helps out when the groom is in need of moral support or words of wisdom or assistance of any kind.

The Ushers

- Collect discarded programs and articles from the pews after the ceremony
- Direct guests to the reception and hand out preprinted maps and directions to those who need them

- 🪶 Assist in gathering the wedding party for photographs
- 🪶 Arrive at the wedding location early to help with setup
- 🪶 Attend to last-minute tasks such as lighting candles, tying bows on reserved rows of seating, etc.
- 🪶 Escort guests to their seats
- 🪶 Roll out aisle runner immediately before processional
- 🪶 Help decorate newlyweds' car (optional)

The Head Usher

- 🪶 Participates in all of the aforementioned ushers' duties
- 🪶 Is responsible for organizing ushers' activities
- 🪶 Makes sure the ushers know their duties and are on time

Am I supposed to pay for lodging for out-of-town attendants?

If your attendants are coming from a distance to be in your wedding, you should try to arrange for them to stay with another friend or family member. If alternate housing is not available, you should pay for rooms at a nearby hotel. But if your attendant would rather stay at a hotel than with your Aunt Martha, she should pay for the hotel herself. Don't offer to put the attendants up with you; things will be crazy enough without worrying about being hospitable to houseguests.

Is it OK to have an honor attendant who lives out of town?

While the honor attendant does have considerable responsibility before the wedding, you shouldn't let distance stop you from having your best friend as your maid of honor. Keep in mind that an out-of-town maid of honor won't be there to help you with as much prewedding planning as would someone who lives locally.

I have a close friend whom I would love to make a bridesmaid. Unfortunately, she has a tendency to act irresponsibly. What should I do?

If you have doubts about the dependability of any of the friends and family on your list of potential wedding party members, think twice before you ask them. It could be an awful strain on the relationship if you had to take back your offer because someone turned out to be more a headache than a help. And it would be a big strain on you to end up having to worry bout whether everything is going to come off smoothly if you opt to hold on to the person. Try to be diplomatic by explaining to your friend that although she was tops on your short list, you knew that she was too busy to play the role of bridesmaid. Also, you can offer to let her fulfill a lesser responsibility, such as performing a reading at the ceremony.

What do I do if one of my attendants isn't fulfilling her duties?

Give her the benefit of the doubt. After all, maybe your maid of honor thought your mom would want to address wedding invitations for you. Perhaps you could copy a list of attendants' duties out of a bridal magazine and give it to all your attendants so as not to single anyone out. If even this doesn't work, try talking to her. Maybe she has other things going on in her life that are preventing her from helping you out. But unless her behavior is extreme, you're going to have to just grin and bear it.

I Thought Everyone Wanted to Be a Bridesmaid

Though it may be hard to believe, some people actually turn down this opportunity to shell out hundreds of dollars on a dress and shoes that they'll wear only once. If this happens to you, be gracious and understand that your friend probably has a good reason for declining your offer.

How do I respond if a friend says no because she can't afford it?

If she's a really good friend and it's in your budget, you could offer to pay for a portion or all of her expenses. Just don't let the other bridesmaids know, or they could go on strike and demand payment for their dresses, too. Your other option is to give her a part in your wedding that is less costly, like that of a reader.

What should I do if one of my attendants balks after finding out the price of the dress?

When you ask your bridesmaids to be in the wedding, tactfully explain to them the costs involved. Say something like, "I'll try to keep the cost of the dress down. It'll probably be in the $150–$200 range." This gives bridesmaids an opportunity to voice concerns up front and, if they decide the costs will be too much for them, drop out. Once she has agreed to be in your wedding, a bridesmaid has no choice but to pay for the dress.

What should I do if a bridesmaid accepts and then drops out at the last minute?

Depending on how close to the wedding date she drops out, you can either go with one less bridesmaid or ask someone else to fill in. The attendant who dropped out should have to pay for the canceled dress order. The replacement attendant would then pay for her own dress, with you paying for any rush charges. If the attendant had to drop out for reasons beyond her control, you should offer to reimburse her for the dress.

CHAPTER FOUR

Outfitting Yourself
and the
Wedding Party

*I*f you thought shopping for dresses to wear to your friends' and relatives' weddings was tough, you've not seen anything yet. Finding the right clothes for your wedding party can be a hassle, to say the least. It's not a matter of figuring out what clothes are appropriate; the type of ceremony you're planning will dictate that. Instead, the biggest problems lie with finding an affordable, flattering dress that all of your bridesmaids will love, convincing your fiancé to wear tails, and most importantly, finding a wedding dress without having a nervous breakdown!

If you're the type who aims to please all of the people all of the time, you might find that this is one case that warrants an exception. While you might spend hours, nay days, contemplating what gifts to buy your nearest and dearest on birthdays and holidays, your first priority on your wedding day is you. Forget all that stuff your friend Bunny has said about how pink wreaks havoc on her complexion, and never mind Lisa's claims that anything in an autumn shade makes her look 10 pounds heavier, your color scheme cannot and will not be all things to all people. So, while taking others' wishes into consideration is all well and good, bending over backwards to make everyone happy is ill-advised.

The Bride

If you thought finding a bathing suit was hard, wait until you start looking for your wedding gown. For most brides, your wedding gown is the most important—and expensive—piece of clothing you'll ever buy. You can feel an enormous amount of pressure to find that "perfect" gown, and this pressure is only heightened by a dozen people telling you what is or isn't appropriate to wear.

Although you know full well that come wedding day all eyes will be on you, appraising your dress and your sense of style, there is no reason to panic. After all, you've got plenty of time to comparison shop. It's not as if you waited until the week before the wedding to go gown shopping . . . . now *that* would be a cause for concern.

My wedding is in 18 months and I want to start looking for my wedding dress already, but my friends are telling me that I should wait. Is that true?

Absolutely not! While your wedding dress doesn't need to be ordered until about six months before the wedding, it's never too early for you to start looking. If you start your search right away, you can get a better idea of the different styles and fabrics available, and which style of gown looks best on you. Also, you probably won't feel as pressured during your search. If you're considering having a dress made, this is the perfect time to begin looking, since custom-made dresses usually take about a year to produce. But if you're planning on losing some weight before your wedding, it's a good idea to wait until you've lost a few pounds before looking for your dress. Otherwise, you may end up spending a small fortune on alterations.

I'm getting married in an outdoor, afternoon ceremony. I found a gown with a cathedral-length train that I absolutely adore. Is this appropriate?

Not really. Cathedral-length trains are considered very formal (think Princess Di), and afternoon weddings are traditionally less formal than evening weddings. In general, brides have fewer style restrictions to remember when shopping than do grooms. Basically, the length of the gown's train and veil determines how formal the gown is; long, cathedral-length trains are best suited for a very formal evening wedding, while shorter chapel or sweep trains are appropriate for less formal daytime or evening weddings. Also, you should buy a gown appropriate to the season in which you're getting married; you probably wouldn't be comfortable wearing long sleeves in July or an off-the-shoulder gown in December.

Many of you probably witnessed the Prince Charles-Lady Di wedding while you were still in your crucial formative years. Ever since, when talk turned to weddings, all you could think about was that glorious train. Call it train fever if you like, but a lot of women are dead set on recreating that Buckingham Palace look, consequences be damned. Of course, a large part of looking like a royal is carrying yourself with poise and dignity—two things you can kiss good-bye if you're planning on sporting a 20 foot train at a backyard ceremony. Keep the following train guidelines in mind when picking out yours:

Lengths:
The Sweep train — Falls around six inches on the floor and worn for semiformal occasions.

The Chapel train — Can fall as much as 22 inches on the floor. This is the most popular choice for today's brides.

The Cathedral train — Usually reserved for very formal affairs, this choice is for those who want the type of train that will effectively fill their limo and finishes entering the room five minutes after they arrive. The Cathedral train falls 22 inches or more on the floor.

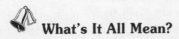

What's It All Mean?

**"Something Old, Something New,
Something Borrowed, Something Blue"**
The odds are pretty high that you'll be wearing all
the above on your wedding day. But do you know
why? The old is to stand for a bride's ties to her past;
the new represents her hope for the future; the borrowed means friendship; and the blue is for faithful-
ness. These things are only significant symbolically,
but try to get a bride to the altar without them.

Styles:
The attached train — Flows out from the back end of
    the gown skirt
A Wateau — Flows from the back yoke
A Capelot — Flows from the back shoulder
A detachable train — Falls from the waistline and can
    be, you guessed it, detached

**My fiancé's mother was hurt that I didn't bring
her along to look for my gown. Was I wrong in
excluding her?**
    You aren't required to bring anyone along with you
when you look for a dress. Most brides take along their
mother or maid of honor when looking for wedding gowns.
You don't want too many people coming with you, though;
their conflicting tastes and opinions may drive you crazy.
    Of course, since your shopping companions are there
to help you, your best bet is to bring along someone
whose fashion sense you trust and admire. It makes no

difference whatsoever if this person is not part of your wedding party, they need only be willing to accompany you on your quest for the right dress. Remember, if you try to please everyone, you'll never settle on anything, so stick with one person you trust. You can always ask your mother-in-law, or a sister who wasn't a part of the search, to accompany you to one of your fittings.

I'm a 40 year-old bride. This will be the first marriage for both me and my fiancé. Can I still wear a traditional white gown?

Of course! A mature, first-time bride can still have a big, splashy wedding and wear a formal, white wedding dress. Designers are constantly creating gowns that look more stylish and elegant than ever, so you don't have to worry about looking like a little girl.

I don't like the idea of wearing a veil over my face. Is this necessary?

What you are talking about is called a blusher, and in most cases, it isn't necessary. However, some religions do require that the face be covered at some point during the ceremony, so check with your officiant before deciding against a blusher.

If I'm wearing a sleeveless gown, should I wear gloves?

Generally, elbow-length gloves are worn if the dress has short sleeves or is sleeveless. Otherwise, short gloves are worn. This goes for bridesmaids, too. If you decide to wear short gloves, you can take one off during the exchanging of rings; with long gloves, split the seam of the

What's it all mean?

The Veil

Veils were originally meant to symbolize the virgin bride's innocence and modesty. These days, our society considers the veil a purely romantic custom. But in parts of the Middle East and Asia, the veil is still used to hide the bride's face completely. The first lace veil is said to have been worn by a woman named Nelly Curtis, George Washington's adopted daughter who married one of his aides. Apparently, the first time the aide ever saw her she was behind a lace curtain. He was mesmerized by her beauty. Nelly, the story goes, made herself a lace veil for the ceremony inn an effort to duplicate the effect.

glove for your ring finger. The seam can be restitched later. If you choose to wear your gloves during the reception, they can be left on at all times except when you're eating.

The Bridesmaids

Traditionally, bridesmaids' dresses have the reputation for being, er, unattractive, to say the least. Thankfully, those days are over. As any glance through a bridal magazine will show you, bridesmaids' dresses can be tasteful, simple, and even elegant. Today, the trickiest part of finding a bridesmaids' dress is choosing the bridesmaids to fill it.

One of my bridesmaids is angry that she didn't get to pick out her dress. Was I wrong in choosing dresses for my bridesmaids?

No! You should take into consideration your brides-maids' tastes when picking out a dress, but they don't have final approval over what they wear. This is your wedding, and it should reflect your taste. But on the other hand, you shouldn't pick out a dress when you know everyone will hate it. Your best bet is to look through bridal magazines with your bridesmaids to get a general feel for the styles they prefer, and then take that information into considera-tion when shopping. Naturally, you should take your maid of honor or another bridesmaid along. After all, someone needs to try on all those dresses!

I want my bridesmaids to wear emerald green dresses. Is this appropriate for a summertime wedding?

Yes! You shouldn't be afraid to choose bridesmaids' dresses in your favorite color just because someone told you it wasn't right for the season. However, the dresses should be in a fabric and style appropriate to the season. Don't dress your bridesmaids in velvet if you're getting married in July, and don't have them wear short sleeves in March.

How do I arrange fittings for an out-of-town attendant?

You should ask your bridesmaid for her measurements so that you can order her dress along with your other bridesmaids'. Once the dress comes in, send it to her so that she can have alterations done at a bridal salon in her city. Don't ask your bridesmaid to order a dress at her own bridal salon. All of the dresses should be ordered together so that they come from the same dye lot; other-wise, the shades of color may vary.

Can bridesmaids wear black?

Since black is traditionally associated with death and mourning, it is generally considered inappropriate for weddings. An exception would be if you're planning an Art Deco wedding, in which case everyone in the wedding party would wear black and white.

One of my attendants is much shorter than the others. How do I find a dress that will flatter everyone?

If you're having a hard time finding a dress that looks great on all of your bridesmaids, you might want to consider having them wear coordinating styles of gowns in the same color. This way, you won't have to worry about one of your bridesmaids feeling uncomfortable in a dress that looks fabulous on everyone else. Alternately, your bridesmaids can wear the same style gown but in complementary colors to create a rainbow effect.

I was told that the junior bridesmaid and flower girl should wear the same dress as the bridesmaids. Is this true?

A junior bridesmaid can wear the same dress as the other bridesmaids, or a different style that is appropriate for her age. A flower girl will probably be too young to wear the same style dress as the bridesmaids; she should wear a dress that is the same color or complements the color and style of the other dresses. And because of their age, it's also appropriate for flower girls to wear a white or cream-colored dress in the same fabric as the other dresses.

The Groom and Ushers

In choosing wedding attire, men experience considerably less stress than their female counterparts. That's because, quite simply, they don't really have as many choices to make. Your wedding's style generally dictates what your fiancé and his ushers will wear, but, of course, nothing is written in stone. For instance, your fiancé wouldn't wear a white tie and tails at a semiformal afternoon wedding; that outfit would be worn only if you were having a very formal evening wedding.

When should my fiancé reserve his clothing?

Your fiancé and the other men in the wedding party should go to a formalwear shop about a month before their wedding in order to reserve their attire. If you're getting married during the peak season between April and October, they should go a little earlier.

What if one of the ushers lives in another city or state?

He should go to a tuxedo shop in his area to be measured, and then pass that information along to the groom so that his tuxedo can be reserved along with the rest of the ushers'.

Should each tuxedo or suit match exactly?

Yes! All the men in the wedding party should wear the same style and color attire. If the men are wearing tuxedos, the groom often wears a different color bow-tie and cummerbund than the rest of the men. Also, the groom wears a different flower in his boutonnière to distinguish himself from the rest of the wedding party.

What should the little guys wear?

Junior ushers, ringbearers, and pages should match the rest of the men in the wedding party. If you want them to look extra cute, have them wear dress shorts or knickers. But keep in mind that a four-year-old may not be comfortable in a minituxedo; children of that age can wear coordinated children's clothing instead.

The Mothers

Your mother, along with your fiancé's mother, will probably spend a great deal of time worrying about what to wear. After all, as hostesses, they want to look their best for their children's wedding. Traditionally, your mother buys her gown first, in keeping with the style and colors of your wedding. She then consults your future mother-in-law, who in turn chooses a gown that complements your mother's in color and style.

Someone told me the mothers' dresses were supposed to match. Is this true?

The mothers' dresses don't have to match exactly, but they should be complementary in color, style, and length. For instance, your future mother in-law shouldn't buy a long, beaded gown when your mother is planning to wear a short dress or evening suit.

My fiancé's mother wants to wear a white dress! How can I tell her I'd prefer her to wear a different color?

Unless you're having an Art Deco (black and white) wedding, the mothers of the bride and groom shouldn't wear white. That color is usually reserved for the bride. Talk to your future mother-in-law about her color choice. Since she was a bride once, too, she should understand your wishes.

The Fathers

Unlike their wives, the fathers of the bride and groom don't really have much choice in the matter of clothing. Again, what your father and your fiancé's father wear depends on the type of wedding you're having. They should get their wedding attire at the same formalwear shop as your fiancé and his wedding party about a month before the wedding. If your father or your fiancé's father lives out of town, he should give his measurements to you so his tuxedo can be ordered along with the others.

Should the fathers' clothes match the other men in the wedding party?

Yes! The style and color of the fathers' clothes should match that of the other male attendants. But if the groom's attendants are wearing bow ties and cummerbunds to match the bridesmaid's dresses, the fathers can just wear a plain black tie and cummerbund if they prefer. However, the fathers usually wear the same flower for a boutonnière as the rest of the men in the wedding party.

The When, What, and Why of Formal, Semiformal, and Informal Dress

Formal, semiformal, and informal are the three key words that dictate the style of the wedding, and all other decisions will flow from the choice you make. A church wedding may be formal, a club wedding semiformal, and a home wedding informal. Other factors are time of day, season of the year, and, finally, the expense, not just for the immediate wedding party, but also for the guests.

Very Formal

- Typically held in a church, synagogue, or luxury hotel
- Two hundred or more guests
- Engraved invitations with traditional typeface and wording
- Bride and groom each have between 4 and 12 attendants
- Bride wears a floor-length gown, cathedral-length train, full-length veil, and long sleeves/arm-covering gloves
- Groom wears cutaway or tails
- Bridesmaids wear matching floor-length dresses or gowns
- Male attendants wear matching cutaway or tails
- Guests don formal attire (white tie for evening)
- Elaborate sit-down dinner, usually held in a ballroom
- Orchestra or live band
- Cascade bouquets and elaborate floral displays
- Limousines or antique cars

Formal

- Typically held in a church, synagogue or luxury hotel
- One hundred or more guests
- Engraved or printed invitations with traditional wording
- Bride and groom each have between three and six attendants
- Bride wears a floor-length gown, chapel-length or sweeping train, fingertip veil or hat, and gloves
- Groom wears cutaway or tails
- Bridesmaids wear matching floor-length dresses or gowns
- Male attendants wear matching cutaway or tails
- Guests wear formal attire or evening wear (black tie for evenings)
- Sit-down dinner or buffet, usually held in a ballroom, banquet facility, or private club
- Live band or disc jockey
- Medium sized bouquets and floral displays
- Limousines, antique cars, or horse-drawn carriages

Semiformal

- Held in a church, synagogue, private home, outdoors, or other location
- Fewer than one hundred guests
- Printed invitations with traditional or personalized wording
- Bride and groom each have between one and three attendants
- Bride wears a floor- or cocktail-length gown with a fingertip veil or hat
- Groom wears a tuxedo, sack coat, or a suit and tie

- ❦ Bridesmaids wear matching floor- or cocktail-length dresses
- ❦ Male attendants wear matching tuxes or suits and ties
- ❦ Guests wear evening or business dress
- ❦ Reception including a simple meal or light refreshments usually held at ceremony location, or at a club, garden, restaurant or home
- ❦ Live band or disc jockey
- ❦ Small bouquet for the bride, simple flower arrangements for decorations

Informal

- ❦ Daytime ceremony often held at home or in a judge's chambers
- ❦ Fewer than 50 guests
- ❦ Printed or hand-written invitations with personalized wording
- ❦ Bride and groom each have one attendant
- ❦ Bride wears a simple gown, suit, or cocktail-length dress, with no veil or train
- ❦ Groom wears a dark business suit and tie
- ❦ Maid/matron of honor wears a street-length dress
- ❦ Best man wears a suit and tie
- ❦ Reception including a simple meal or light refreshments, usually held at home, at site of ceremony, or at a restaurant
- ❦ Corsage or small bouquet for the bride, simple flower arrangements for decorations

CHAPTER FIVE

Party Time: Bridal Showers and Other Prewedding Parties

O nce you've chosen your bridesmaids, registered for gifts, started the battle of the guest list, and convinced your father that a backyard barbecue wasn't exactly the kind of reception you had in mind, your female relatives and friends will probably start talking about showers. These little gatherings, in which your friends "shower" you and your fiancé with carefully chosen items from your registry, are usually held long after the dust from your engagement party has settled, but not later than two weeks before the wedding.

Quite probably the best thing about these parties is that you have no hand in their organizing, planning, and arranging. Perhaps it is the only time during this hectic period in your life that you are going to be feted without having to worry about so much as one pesky logistic. While some questions of etiquette are bound to crop up, the showers are your moments to relax and bask in the glory of complete and total freedom from responsibility.

My maid of honor and I agreed to have a wedding shower. Should I let her take care of everything or do I have any responsibilities that I should know about?

You are expected to help your maid of honor by asking how many people she is thinking of inviting and then providing her with a guest list that roughly matches that number. Keep in mind that it's better to invite a few extra people in case some can't make it. Also provide your maid/matron of honor with the names and locations of the stores where you're registered for gifts so that she can spread the word to the guests.

Is my fiancé allowed at the shower?

Although spending an afternoon with a roomful of women eating little sandwiches may not be your beloved's idea of a fun time, it's a good idea if your fiancé is there; after all, the purpose of a shower is to give presents to both you and your future husband. But if the shower is scheduled for the same day as the Super Bowl, it's OK to let him stay home.

Can my mother host a wedding shower?

Traditionally, your mother or grandmother should not host a shower; that responsibility should be left to more distant relatives, like a cousin or aunt, or to the maid of honor, bridesmaids, and other friends. Also, the gurus of etiquette frown upon the groom's immediate family hosting a shower as well, but this is becoming more and more common today. The logic behind this "rule" is that the bride and groom's families shouldn't appear to be asking for gifts for the bride. This is also why it's acceptable to list where you're registered on the shower, but not wedding, invitation.

My sister is my maid of honor. In this case, who should host the wedding shower?

Since so many women choose to have a sister as their honor attendant, it's now commonplace for the sister of the bride to host a wedding shower. Naturally, the other bridesmaids can be cohostesses of the shower.

Is it OK to have more than one bridal shower?

It's common to have more than one shower. Sometimes the honor attendant will throw one for the bride's friends and family, and then a member of the groom's family will throw one for her friends and relatives. Often, the bride's coworkers will have another shower for her at the office.

Who Are All These People?

Like the wedding itself, some people believe the shower to be little more than a way to get more stuff for the bride and groom (on second thought, maybe that's true). Seriously though, a bridal shower wasn't meant to be an elaborate affair with dozens and dozens of guests. As with the wedding, guest lists should be limited to only those people who are close to the bride and groom.

Should I invite the same people to more than one shower?

The only people who should go to more than one shower are the bride and groom's mothers and the attendants. They shouldn't be expected to buy presents for each shower—just one will suffice. For all other potential guests, ask your hostesses to compare guest lists before sending out invitations. If others are invited to more than one shower, they may feel obligated to buy you more than one gift.

I heard that my coworkers are planning a wedding shower for me. What should I expect?

Often, coworkers will want to help you celebrate your impending wedding, even if you couldn't invite them to the big event. They'll probably throw it on one of your last days at work prior to the wedding. Normally, the coworker shower involves colleagues gathering together, often on lunch hour or right after work, feasting on refreshments (cake, cookies, fruit, tea, soft drinks, etc.) and presenting a group gift.

Can we invite guests to the shower who aren't invited to the wedding?

With few exceptions, you really shouldn't. If you're having a small wedding exclusively with your immediate families, or getting married a great distance from where you live, your friends may decide to throw you a shower anyway. Also, your coworkers will probably throw you a small shower at work without expecting to go to your wedding. But in general, you shouldn't expect people to buy you a gift without asking them to share in the celebration of your marriage.

My mother-in-law wants to have a huge shower at a reception hall, inviting every woman from the guest list. Is this necessary?

No. Showers are supposed to be small and intimate. There's no need to invite every female on the guest list. Only those friends and family members close to the bride need to be included. Try to talk to your mother-in-law about trimming her guest list; if she's insistent, suggest having two or more smaller showers instead.

What is the suggested wording for bridal shower invitations?

Here is a perfectly valid sample:

Please join us for
a Bridal Shower in honor of
Brooke Jennifer Anderson
on Sunday, the seventeenth of June
at one o'clock in the afternoon
Lindo Restaurant
123 West Fifth Avenue
New York, New York
(Hostess Name/s)

I live in Dallas, but many of my best childhood friends are from Chicago, my hometown. They're all invited to the wedding, but I'm wondering if I should send them shower invitations even though I know they won't be able to attend?

In such cases, a shower invitation can function a lot like a post card, letting your friends know that you wish they were right there with you. What's more, sending shower invitations to friends in distant places is a great way to make them feel included in the festivities and build up anticipation for the actual wedding day.

My matron of honor, my only attendant, lives three time zones away from me. The rest of my friends are also spread out all over the country. Since she still wants to throw me a shower, can we do it the day before the wedding, once everyone's in town?

Expecting your friends to travel great distances for a bridal shower is asking for a great deal, so staging the shower immediately prior to the wedding is a wonderful idea. Your matron of honor could even arrange to have a bachelorette-party-themed shower the night before the wedding, providing you with the ideal opportunity to have fun and blow off some steam before tying the knot.

I know that its proper to write thank-you notes for wedding presents, but what about shower presents?

Anytime one receives a present, etiquette dictates that a thank-you note be sent as a show appreciation. This is a given. Some wedding showers, however, have witnessed guests being asked to write their name and address on an envelope under the guise of "signing in." After the shower, the bride then fills these envelopes with thank you cards and dispatches them accordingly. As convenient as this sounds, such a practice falls directly under the heading of "rude" and should not be practiced if the rules of etiquette are of any import whatsoever.

Can we have a co-ed party instead?

If one or both of you has a lot of friends of the opposite sex, there's no reason why you can't have a party that includes men and women. This kind of party is usually called a "Jack and Jill" shower, and the hostess should try to avoid gender-specific activities. Men usually aren't as enthusiastic about shower games and the like as women, so "Jack and Jills" have a tendency to turn into regular parties. Some couples even decide to have them in addition to or instead of the bachelor or bachelorette party. In this instance, the bride and groom and their friends will all go out to a bar or nightclub together.

Is it proper to invite the officiant to the co-ed party and reception?

Don't invite the officiant to the co-ed party but not only is inviting the officiant to the reception proper, but etiquette actually demands it. Whether you pick a judge or a member of the clergy to do the honors, whether you know them well or not at all, you should make some room on the guest list. To be sure, if your officiant doesn't know you very well, he or she may very well send regrets, but extending an invitation is a matter of course.

Bridesmaid Teas and Other Sordid Affairs

After you've unwrapped your last shower gift, it's time for you to start getting ready for the most important party of your life—the bachelorette party! (Just kidding!)

Who is in charge of the bachelor/bachelorette party?

The maid of honor, together with the other bridesmaids, is in charge of the bachelorette party, while the best man and ushers organize the bachelor party.

What can I do to show my appreciation to the people who throw me engagement parties and showers? Is it appropriate to send a gift?

Believe it or not, gifts are rarely a bad idea. While thank-you notes should suffice when responding to engagement and shower presents, feel free to go the extra mile for those who actually go to the trouble and expense of throwing parties in your honor. Show your gratitude and thoughtfulness by sending both a thank-you note and a small gift, such as flowers, a bottle of wine, a gift basket, fancy teas, or a coffee sampler.

When should the bachelor/bachelorette parties be held?

In days of yore, these grand affairs were held the night before the wedding. But now they're usually held a week or two before the ceremony, thus ensuring that the members of the wedding party will be fully recovered from their hangovers in time for the wedding.

My maid of honor has asked everyone to pitch in money for the bachelorette party. Is this OK?

Since bachelorette party guests are not expected to bring gifts, it's perfectly all right to ask for contributions—as long as all the invitees are told about the plans and financial arrangements in advance.

I think bachelor/bachelorette parties are tacky. Do we need to have them?

According to tradition, sometime before the wedding, friends of the bride and groom should take them out (separately, of course) for one last evening of, er, revelry. These parties are by no means mandatory, but your single friends might be disappointed if you don't want one. Furthermore, they will probably throw one for you anyway. Just tell your friends (and have your fiancé tell his friends) that you would prefer something a little more dignified than getting drunk and watching scantily clad men or women dance around on tables.

Should I take my bridesmaids out before the wedding?

It's customary for the bride to take her bridesmaids out for tea in appreciation for all they've done for her. Since not many people go out for tea anymore, many brides treat their bridesmaids to lunch or dinner several days before the wedding. If you're getting married in the late afternoon or evening and are feeling exceptionally calm, you can take your bridesmaids out for a nice brunch the morning of the wedding.

The bridesmaids' tea and the bridal shower sound kind of similar. Wouldn't having a two-for-one simplify matters?

Not at all. While all sorts of friends are invited to the wedding shower, and the bride is showered with gifts, the bridesmaids' tea/luncheon is a chance for the bride and her attendants to hang out together and show their gratitude in the hectic days before the wedding. Nobody else attends. Usually, the tea or luncheon is held on the weekend before the wedding so working girls need not miss out.

With everything that needs to be done, I don't think I'll be able to fit the bridesmaids' luncheon in at the last minute. Can I schedule it two or, better yet, three weeks before the wedding?

This is your wedding, and of course, there are a million little things that you have to do to make the big day perfect for you and your guests. Your bridesmaids, however, have selflessly given of their time and money to make sure that your wedding goes smoothly. Since the only thing in it for them is your happiness (and perhaps a return on the favor come their wedding day), we recommend that you do everything in your power to clear a few hours in your schedule and make everything perfect for all the attendants who have done so much to support you in your hour of need. Holding a lunch a week before the wedding will show how much you appreciate all of their efforts (unless, of course, there are bridesmaids coming in from out of town, in which case you should plan the luncheon for a time when all your bridesmaids can be in attendance—even if that means holding it on the day of the wedding itself).

What's It All Mean?

The Bridal Shower –

This custom is believed to have started in Holland, where legend has it that a disapproving father would not provide his daughter with a dowry so that she might marry a less-than-wealthy miller. Her friends provided her with the then-essential dowry by "showering" her with gifts.

Is it customary to buy bridesmaids presents as tokens of appreciation?

Yes. Just as the bridesmaids may choose to give their joint gift to the bride at the bridesmaids' tea, the bride bestows individual gifts upon her bridesmaids at this very same event. After all these women have done, giving a little party and a few presents is the least a bride could do.

What is this bridesmaids cake I've been hearing about?

This is a fun tradition that's basically a variation on the bouquet toss theme. Baked inside the usually pink bridesmaids cake is a silver ring tied to a ribbon. Whichever bridesmaid gets the piece with the ring is the one who will be the first to the altar. You can either buy the ring and ribbon at a specialty shop and bake it into the cake yourself, or you can order the bridesmaids cake from a bakery.

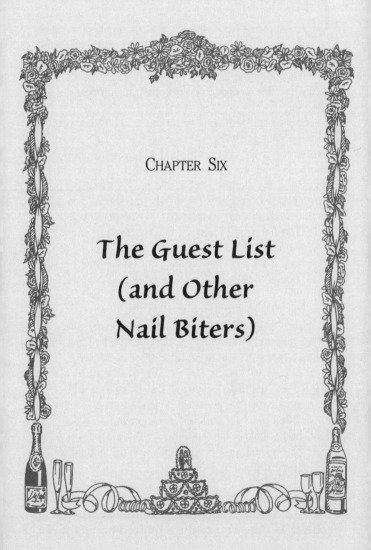

CHAPTER SIX

The Guest List
(and Other
Nail Biters)

C ompiling your guest list can be a smooth, effort-lessly enjoyable process—that is, if you have a ten-sion-free family life, an endless supply of wedding funds, unlimited reception space, and a magician who'll whip up a seating plan that pleases everyone. But if you're not one of the lucky .0001 percent of the population who fits into this category, you may find this process, er, challenging.

You may find it helpful to let the size of your wedding determine your guest list, not vice versa. That's because a guest list has a life of its own, and will grow to enormous proportions if left unchecked. Unfortunately, if you're like most brides, the same can't be said for your budget. So before anyone even utters the words "guest list," you and your fiancé should determine what size wedding you want.

First, you'll need to determine a budget with your fami-lies, which is no mean feat (see Chapter Two for more advice on this issue). Then, taking your budget into consid-eration, decide on the style your wedding will be. You should then be able to make a rough estimate of how many guests you'll be able to accommodate. This way you can tell your parents and future in-laws upfront how many guests they are allocated, rather than finding out too late that you'll need an airplane hangar to accommodate everyone!

How do we divide the guest list between us?

In most cases the guest list is divided evenly between the two families, regardless of who is paying for what. Established couples often split the list three ways: the bride's parents, the groom's parents, and the couple each invite one-third of the guests.

My fiancé and I both come from large families with a tradition of big, fancy weddings. The problem is that we are on a limited budget and

can't afford a dinner reception for our 200 guests. Help!

Relax. There is no rule that states all weddings must be followed by an expensive sit-down meal. Cut costs with a poolside barbecue reception. Or, if you'd prefer something a bit more formal, offer your guests champagne, hors d'oeuvres, and wedding cake to the sound of a jazz band. Morning brunches are also an elegant, less costly alternative. Be creative!

To contain costs, may I invite some people to the ceremony but not the reception?

Yes. You'll need to order separate reception cards that correspond with the invitations to the ceremony. For the guests who will be invited to the ceremony only, simply omit this card.

Do we have to invite our coworkers?

If you work for a large company, inviting your coworkers could be a financial disaster. Even small and midsize companies can take a toll on the wedding budget, if you go the all-inclusive route. A good rule of thumb for extending invitations to coworkers is to invite only those with whom you socialize outside of the immediate work environment.

Should we invite our bosses?

While there is no law of etiquette that would have you invite your boss or supervisor if you do not normally socialize with him/her, extending an invitation to an immediate superior can be a nice gesture if you are inviting other people from work and if office politics are of any concern.

Is it appropriate to hand-deliver wedding invitations to coworkers and supervisors while at the workplace?

No. All invitations, with the possible exception of the parents throwing the wedding, must be sent directly to the homes of the recipients, whether they be coworkers, bosses, or next-door neighbors.

I want to invite my friends from work, but I don't think we can afford to invite all of their spouses as well. Could I include only those spouses whom I already know, and ask the rest of my coworkers to come alone?

Bad idea. Excluding spouses from invitations is simply not done. If you can't afford to invite all your coworkers and their sundry husbands and wives, invite only those colleagues with whom you are on the closest of terms.

We would like to invite many more guests than we can accommodate. Is it okay to do a second invitation mailing if we receive many regrets the first time around?

Absolutely. It's realistic to anticipate some regrets (on average, about 20 to 25 percent of invited guests will be unable to attend). This gives you the opportunity to send invitations to those people on your "wish list." Your first mailing should be sent 10 to 12 weeks before the wedding date; the second should be sent no later than five weeks prior.

It turns out that we have to cut people from our guest list. How do we decide who stays and who goes?

Don't draw names out of a hat and ax anyone whose name is chosen. Instead, establish rules for your list that you, your fiancé, and your respective families agree on, such as a "no coworkers" policy. Remember, apply all rules across the board. Making exceptions for certain people is a good way to offend others and create more headaches for yourself. Following are some policies to consider:

- 🍃 *No children.* The fact that you're not inviting children is usually implied to parents by the fact that their children's names do not appear anywhere on the invitation. Just to be safe, however, make sure your mother (and anyone else who might be questioned) is aware of your policy. What age you choose as a cut-off point between children and young adults is up to you, although both 18 and 16 are common cutoffs.
- 🍃 *No coworkers.* If you were counting on talking to people at the wedding to help strengthen business ties, this may not be the best option. But if you do need to cut somewhere, this may be a good way to go.
- 🍃 *No distant relatives.* If you have a large immediate family and many friends, you may want to exclude distant relatives from the guest list. Again, be consistent. As long as your second cousins don't have to hear that your third cousins twice removed have been invited, they should understand your need to cut costs.

Is it always necessary to invite a guest's "significant other"?

Yes. You should always invite significant others of married guests, engaged guests, and couples who live together. This also holds true for people who are generally considered couples. You may send one invitation to couples who live together, listing their names alphabetically on the envelope. If an engaged couple or "steadies" live apart, send a separate invitation to each. You should never refer to a significant other on an invitation by "and guest."

Is it necessary to invite dates for single guests?

No, but if your budget will allow it, it's a nice gesture. This is especially appropriate for people who may not know many others at the wedding, as it will help them feel more comfortable. But if you can't afford to invite single guests with a date, they will almost certainly understand. To make your single guests feel more comfortable, it's nice to try to seat them at the same table, especially if they're around the same age. Whatever policy you adopt, be sure to apply it across the board; don't let some single guests bring dates and not others. And if some single guests return a response card indicating that two will attend when you invited only one, don't be shy about calling them to politely explain your guest policy.

If a distant relative or acquaintance invited me to his/her wedding, am I obligated to return the favor?

No. Most people will understand if you make them aware that you're cutting costs and having a small affair. If people approach you and assume they're being invited when they're not, be honest with them—and quick. Don't go home and worry for weeks about how to break it to them. Waiting only makes things more awkward, and it also causes people to wonder whether something happened over that time to make you change your mind. The best approach is to be honest right then and there; tell them you'd love to have them, but you're having a small wedding and it is impossible to have everyone. It may be a little awkward, but it beats dashing expectations later.

Divorced Parents

If a divorce between your parents or your groom's parents was amicable, be thankful. You won't have to plan around family tensions. If, however, the relationship between the ex-spouses is best compared to that of the North and South after the American Civil War, you'd better map out a battle plan of your own to deal with it.

My mother, who has recently remarried, assumed that I would not be inviting my natural father to my wedding. Although he and I are not particularly close, it's important to me that he be there. Now my mother is threatening to not attend if my natural father does. What should I do?

You should feel free to invite anyone you choose to your wedding, regardless of family infighting. It is up to each invitee to accept or decline your invitation. This is not something you can control, and trying to do so will only lead to greater headaches. If your mother refuses to attend if your father does, tell her that you're sorry and you will miss her. Chances are, when she realizes you mean it, she'll come around.

My fiancé always seems to be on the verge of fisticuffs with his stepfather. Must we invite him to our wedding?

To invite your fiancé's mother without her husband would be awkward and, well, rude. Doing so would only create more tension between your fiancé and his stepfather, and may offend his mother as well. If the situation is extreme, the stepfather will probably share your discomfort and choose not to attend. On the other hand, if your fiancé insists on excluding his stepfather, he should discuss it first with his natural parent to find out the most tactful way to handle this.

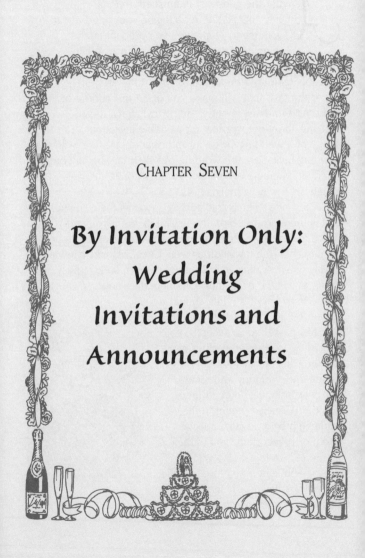

CHAPTER SEVEN

By Invitation Only: Wedding Invitations and Announcements

After the guest list is finished and your fiancé has succeeded in changing your mind about wanting to elope, you will probably start thinking about wedding invitations. While deciding upon the colors and the style of these invites will probably take up a great deal of your time and energy, this is not the task that will wake you up in the middle of the night. And thinking about wedding invitations means thinking about the wording on wedding invitations. The formality of a wedding (even an informal one!) starts with the wedding invitation, the wording of which can be as complicated as contract negotiations for a corporate merger—which, in a way, a marriage is.

The bride's family traditionally sponsors the wedding, and is therefore listed on the invitation, but if you and your fiancé feel strongly about it, you can name stepparents or his family on the invitation as well. Circumstances can vary greatly when dealing with divorced parents, so use these forms as general guidelines. One important note: A deceased parent's name should never appear on an invitation. If one of your parents has passed away recently, you should try to find some other way to honor his or her memory during the ceremony and reception. For instance, you can mention the deceased parent in the wedding program with a special poem or prayer dedicated to their memory. You might also wish to display and light a memorial candle, or put up a flower arrangement during the ceremony.

Traditional/Bride's Parents Sponsor:

Mr. and Mrs. Joseph Moran
request the honor of your presence
at the marriage of their daughter
Margaret Ann
to
Mr. Justin McCannon
Saturday, the third of July
at three o'clock
Holy Trinity Lutheran Church
Chicago, Illinois

Bride and Groom's Parents Sponsor:

Mr. and Mrs. Joseph Moran
and
Mr. and Mrs. Robert McCann
request the honor of your presence
at the marriage of their children
Miss Margaret Ann Moran
and
Mr. Justin James McCann

Traditional/Bride's Parents Sponsor, but Groom's Parents Also Want to Be Listed

Mr. and Mrs. Joseph Morgan
request the honor of your presence
at the marriage of their daughter
Margaret Ann
to
Mr. Justin McCann
son of
Mr. and Mrs. Robert McCann
on Saturday, the third of July
Two thousand and one
at three o'clock
Holy Trinity Lutheran Church
Chicago, Illinois

Groom's Parents Sponsor:

Mr. and Mrs. Robert McCann
request the honor of your presence
at the marriage of Miss Margaret Ann Moran
to their son
Mr. Justin James McCann

Bride and Groom Sponsor:

The honor of your presence is requested
at the marriage of
Miss Margaret Ann Moran
and
Mr. Justin James McCann

or

Miss Margaret Ann Moran
and
Mr. Justin James McCann
request the honor of your presence
at their marriage

Bride's Mother, Not Remarried, Sponsors:

Mrs. Patricia Moran
requests the honor of your presence
at the marriage of her daughter
Margaret Ann

Bride's Mother, Remarried, Sponsors:

Mrs. Patricia Clark
requests the honor of your presence
at the marriage of her daughter
Margaret Ann Moran

Bride's Mother and Stepfather Sponsor:
Mr. and Mrs. Michael Clark
request the honor of your presence
at the marriage of her daughter
Margaret Ann Moran

Bride's Father, not Remarried, Sponsors:
Mr. Joseph Moran
requests the honor of your presence
at the marriage of his daughter
Margaret Ann

Bride's Father, Remarried, Sponsors:
Mr. and Mrs. Joseph Moran
request the honor of your presence
at the marriage of his daughter
Margaret Ann

Bride's Divorced Parents Issue Invitation Together:
Mrs. Patricia Clark
and
Mr. Joseph Moran
request the honor of your presence
at the marriage of their daughter
Margaret Ann Moran

Second Marriage (Divorcee uses a combo of maiden & married names)
Mr. and Mrs. Joseph Morgan
request the honor of your presence
at the marriage of their daughter
Margaret Ann Morgan Harrison

Invitations Issued by More Than Two Sets of Parents

Mr. and Mrs. Joseph Morgan
Mr. and Mrs. Robert McCann
and
Mrs. and Mrs. Andrew C. White
request the honor of your presence
at the marriage of their children

One Parent Deceased (Living parent not remarried)

Mrs. Joseph Morgan
requests the honor of your presence
at the marriage of her daughter
Margaret Ann

One Parent Deceased (Living Parent has remarried)

Mr. and Mrs. James L. Pearl
request the honor of your presence
at the marriage of her daughter
Margaret Ann Morgan

or (if new parent has adopted the daughter)

Mr. and Mrs. James L. Pearl
request the honor of your presence
at the marriage of their daughter
Margaret Ann Morgan

Close Relative Sponsors (Both parents deceased)

Mr. and Mrs. Frederick Morgan
Request the honor of your presence
At the marriage of their granddaughter
Margaret Ann Morgan

Bride and Groom Have Children

Margaret Ann Morgan
and
Justin James McCann
Together with their children
Jennifer C. McCann, Michael D. Morgan, and
Elizabeth A. Morgan
invite you to share with them
a celebration of love.
Their marriage will take place
on Saturday, the third of July
at three o'clock
Holy Trinity Lutheran Church
Chicago, Illinois

Not Indicating Names of Parents

Together with their parents
Margaret Ann Morgan
and
Justin James McCann
request the honour of your presence
as they are united in marriage
on Saturday, the third of July
at three o'clock

Religious Ceremonies

If you want to emphasize the religious aspect of marriage, it's best to check with the officiant before printing invitations; wording will be different according to affiliations.

Protestant:

Mr. and Mrs. Joseph Moran
are pleased to invite you
to join in a Christian celebration
of the marriage of their daughter
Margaret Ann Moran

Catholic:

Mr. and Mrs. Joseph Moran
request the honor of your presence
at the Nuptial Mass
at which their daughter
Margaret Ann
and
Justin James McCann
will be united in the Sacrament of Holy Matrimony

Jewish:

Mr. and Mrs. Jeremy Green
and
Mr. and Mrs. Michael Cohen
request the honor of your presence
at the marriage of their children
Catharine Susan
to
William Samuel

Traditional Jewish invitations name
the groom's parents as well as the bride's.

Also, many Jewish couples decide to spice up their invitations with transliterated Hebrew or Yiddish words. Inviting guests to join in celebrating the simcha of their wedding is growing more and more common.

Military Ceremonies

In military weddings, rank determines the placement of names. If the person's rank is lower than sergeant, omit the rank, but list the branch of service of which the bride or groom is a member. Junior officer's titles are placed below their names and are followed by their branch of service. If the rank is higher than lieutenant, titles are placed before names and the branch of service is placed on the following line. Check with the specific branch's protocol officer if you have particular questions.

For those whose rank is lower than sergeant:
Mr. and Mrs. Roger Parker
request the honor of your presence
at the marriage of their daughter
Beth Elaine
United States Army
to
Justin James Clark

For junior officers:
Mr. and Mrs. Roger Parker
request the honor of your presence
at the marriage of their daughter
Beth Elaine
to
Justin James Clark
First Lieutenant, United States Navy

For those with a rank higher than lieutenant:

Mr. and Mrs. Roger Parker
Request the honor of your presence
at the marriage of their daughter
Beth Elaine
to
Captain Justin James Clarke
United States Navy

Who, What, Where, When, and Why

Invitations should be ordered after you've determined the date, times, and sites of the ceremony and reception, but not before the guest list is finalized, about two to three months prior to the wedding. And remember, you'll be addressing these by hand, so you'll want to order some extras in case you make a mistake. Also, if you have any "standby" guests, you'll need the extras to send out.

What should we include with the invitation?

Along with the wedding invitation, most people include a separate reception card, which lists where and when the reception will be held, and a response card, which tells you whether or not the invitee will be able to come. The party paying for the reception is listed as sponsor on the reception card:

Mr. and Mrs. Joseph Moran
request the pleasure of your company
Saturday, the third of July
at six o'clock
Fairview Country Club
1638 Eastview Lane
Chicago, Illinois.

For less formal weddings, you can simply write:

Reception
immediately following the ceremony
Fairview Country Club
1638 Eastview Lane
Chicago, Illinois.

Response cards allow guests
to check off whether or not they'll
be attending and if they're bringing
a guest. You'll also have three
envelopes: the outer envelope, inner
envelope, and return envelope, which
is already stamped and addressed to
you to facilitate the whole R.S.V.P. process.

Can we cut down on expenses by omitting the postage from the R.S.V.P cards?

Hosts enclose the self-stamped response cards because
these encourage a quick response and can save you a
great deal of time and energy in the final analysis. The initials R.S.V.P. stand for *Respondez s'il vous plait*, which
translates into "respond, if you please" or "please respond,"
and it is the height of rudeness for an invited guest not to
inform the host of his or her intention to attend or decline
a wedding invitation. But without the proper postage, many
people will be tempted to forgo the mailman and call in
their reply via phone.

How does it all go together?

First, lay the response card face up under the flap of
the return envelope. Then, place this and all other inser-
tions, including the reception card and directions (if any)
inside the invitation, and then lay the invitation face up

inside of the inner envelope, which already has the guests' names written on it. Last but not least, insert the inner envelope into the outer envelope so that the handwritten names face the back of the envelope. It's a good idea to weigh the entire invitation before affixing any stamps; most invitations will need extra postage.

Can we use preprinted address labels?

No. Computer-generated address labels on your wedding invitations are a sure way to get yourself on the etiquette police's 10-most-wanted list. Invitations should be written out by hand. If you feel that your handwriting is poor and you have some extra room in your budget, you may want to consider hiring a calligrapher to address your invitations. Otherwise, enlist the help of a friend with beautiful handwriting.

Is there a form we need to follow when writing out invitations?

When you're finalizing your guest list, don't invite too many people who live on boulevards, because abbreviations are not allowed! With the exception of titles such as Mr., Ms., and Dr., all streets, cities, and states should be written out completely; no St., no Ave., no Blvd. On the inside envelope, simply write the titles and last names (Mr. and Mrs. Jones).

How should we address invitations to people with professional titles?

The names should be written on one line, with the person with the title listed first: "Dr. Caroline Smith and Mr. Frederick Smith." The inner envelope would read: "Dr. and Mr. Smith."

If the couple are both medical doctors the envelope should be addressed to "The Doctors Smith. (Note: The title "Dr." should not be used in addressing a Ph.D.—someone

How to Word the Reply Card

The following are three examples of acceptable reply card format. The last of these gives your guests the opportunity to preselect their entrée if a sit-down dinner is on the menu.

Style A
We look forward to celebrating with you
Please respond on or before the first of July
M (or Name) _____
Number of Persons: _____
_____accepts _____regrets

Style B
The favor of a reply is requested
on or before the first of July
M (or Name)_____
Number of Persons:_____
_____accepts _____regrets

Style C
The courtesy of a reply is requested
by the first of July
M_____
Number of persons_____
_____accepts _____regrets
Chicken Florentine_____ Salmon_____

with a doctorate degree—but only a medical doctor, because Ph.D.s are called doctors only in academia, not socially.

When addressing a member of the clergy, the envelope should read:

"The Reverend Jonathan Thomas and Mrs. Thomas."

Do we need to send an invitation to our attendants?
Although a reply is not expected or required, you should send invitations to everybody involved in the wedding as a memento. This includes attendants, siblings, parents, and the officiant, along with their respective significant others. You don't need to send invitations to whoever is issuing the invitation, however. Your parents will probably think their credit card bills are memento enough.

My friends Andrew and Lisa are roommates. Can I send one invitation to both of them?
Your friends should each get a separate invitation—whether or not they live together. The only instance in which you would send two friends the same invitation is if they are romantically involved, or married, and living together.

Whose name comes first when addressing a same-sex couple who live together?

In the case of same-sex couples, names should be listed in alphabetical order. You would also not put their names on the same line (i.e., Mr. John Jones and Mr. Matthew Strong) as this is only done for married couples, but have each name on a separate line.

Final Notes

- 🎵 If sending an invitation to a single woman who's been married before, use "Mrs." regardless of her present marital status. If she's never been married, the proper address is "Miss" not "Ms."
- 🎵 When addressing the inner envelope, you can go one of two ways:
  - A. Use their title and last name (i.e., Mr. and Mrs. Thomas); or
  - B. Use full names (i.e., Michael and Jane Thomas)
- 🎵 Never connect two names with "and" unless the two people are a married couple
- 🎵 If the names are too long to fit on one line, indent the second name under the name on the first line. Do not use more than two lines for listing names.
- 🎵 Never put either "and guest" or "and family" on the invitation, the former is considered rude and impersonal, while the latter denotes the invitee's entire family.

When should the invitations be sent out?

Mail out invitations about eight weeks before the wedding, with an R.S.V.P. date of about three weeks before the wedding. If you're planning a wedding near a holiday, mail out your invitations a few weeks earlier to give your guests some extra time to plan. This should also give you plenty of time to give a final head count to the caterer. Also, as regrets come in, you can send invitations to those people squeezed off the original guest list.

What (and What Not) to Say

We all know that you're not supposed to list where you're registered on the wedding invitation, right? Good! But many couples encounter situations that they feel might merit a quick mention on the wedding invitations. However, with few exceptions, nothing but the standard date, time, and location of the ceremony should be listed on the actual invitation.

How can we let guests know we'd prefer black tie?

Here's the exception to the rule. The words "Black Tie Invited" at the bottom of your invitation will let guests know that you're planning a formal wedding. That's a signal for your guests to dress to the nines. However, you can't mandate tuxedos, suits, or any other type of dress.

Can we write "No Smoking" on the wedding invitation or reception card?

While it's OK to forbid smoking at your reception for health or other reasons, you shouldn't write that on the invitation. The easiest thing to do is to leave ashtrays off the tables and place small "No Smoking" cards on each table. Unless the reception facility strictly forbids it, however, you should accommodate smoking guests by having a designated smoking area.

Is there a way to indicate on the invitation that children aren't desired at the wedding?

If the child's name isn't written on either the outer or inner envelope (Mr. and Mrs. John Smith, Sara and Andrew), the parents should understand that children aren't welcome at the reception. This is doubly true if the ceremony and reception are at night. But not everybody will understand these subtle hints, so be sure that your mother and anyone else who may be asked is aware of your policy.

How can I spread word of where I'm registered?

Don't let people know by including registry information with the wedding invitation. Guests will generally ask your mother, future mother-in-law, or other family members what you would like. However, it is acceptable to list where you're registered on a bridal shower invitation.

Can we ask for cash instead of gifts?

Although cash is the traditional wedding gift in some parts of the country, you should never request cash on any invitation. If you really do have everything you could possibly need, your family and friends will probably recognize that and give you a check instead. Also, your mother or other family members could discreetly pass the word along when asked for gift ideas or where you're registered.

Some of my guests are not in a position to buy gifts. Can I request that people not buy us gifts by printing "No gifts, please" on the invitation?

Such a request is not proper on an invitation. A hand-written note to specific guests will do the job. Consider writing something to the effect of: "We look forward to seeing you at our wedding, and we are asking our friends not to bring gifts. Your presence in itself will be as fine a gift as we can imagine."

Hear Ye, Hear Ye: Wedding Announcements

If you and your fiancé are like most couples, you were not able to invite everyone on your original guest list; business associates, friends and family living far away, and others may have been squeezed off the list due to budget or space constraints. Wedding announcements are a convenient way to let people know of your recent nuptials. Obviously, they are not sent to anyone who received an invitation to your wedding, even if they were unable to come. Also, you should note that people receiving announcements are under no obligation to buy you a gift.

When should the announcements be sent?

Announcements should be mailed immediately after your wedding. You and your fiancé should have them ready before you leave for your honeymoon; your maid of honor or best man can mail them while you are gone.

What should the announcements say?

The traditional wording of announcements is as follows:

Mr. and Mrs. Joseph Moran
proudly announce
the marriage of their daughter
Margaret Ann
and
Mr. Justin James McCannon
Saturday, the third of July
one thousand nine hundred and
ninety-three
Holy Trinity Lutheran Church
Chicago, Illinois.

Naturally, whoever is named on the invitation as the wedding's sponsor should also be the person or persons announcing the marriage.

Can I send at-home cards with announcements?

Yes. These cards, which let people know your new address and when you'll be moved in, can be included with either invitations or announcements. At-home cards are also an easy way to let people know whether you have taken your husband's name and how you prefer to be addressed after you're married.

When should I submit my wedding announcement if I want it to appear in my local newspaper right after the wedding?

Newspapers print wedding announcements the day after the wedding, but the copy should be submitted two to four weeks in advance. As with engagement announcements, check with the society editor. Some newspapers have begun charging for this service or print the announcements only if they have room.

The wording for the announcement may be terse or verbose. Regardless, this is an opportunity for the bride to go on record by announcing whether she will retain her own last name. If this is not indicated, it should be assumed that she is taking her husband's surname. Newspaper wedding announcements can come with a picture of the bride and groom, and usually read something like this:

Mr. and Mrs. Adam Claypool of Hillandale, Maryland, announce the marriage of their daughter, Justine, to Mr. James Brendan Danielson of Dallas, Texas. Mr. Danielson is the son of Dr. and Mrs. Roger Wakefield Danielson, also of Dallas.

The bride, who will retain her last name of Claypool, is a graduate of the University of Maryland and is a development executive for National Public Radio. The groom was graduated from the Rochester Institute of Technology and is a biochemist with the Naval Ordinance Laboratory.

The couple will reside in Bethesda, Maryland.

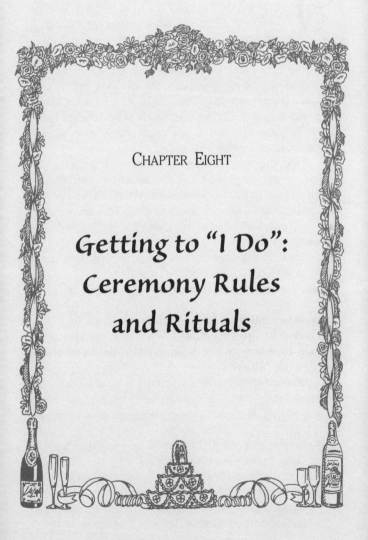

CHAPTER EIGHT

Getting to "I Do": Ceremony Rules and Rituals

he wedding ceremony is an often nerve-wracking experience that takes you from being an engaged couple to being a married couple. Depending upon your personal convictions, this transformation can be a religious or strictly civil (legal) act. If you and your fiancé practice the same faith and are established members of a house of worship, this decision will be easy for you. If you practice different faiths or have been inactive, you may find this decision much more difficult. Take your time, and choose the type of ceremony you want with a great deal of care and forethought.

If you decide on a religious ceremony, consult the officiant of your choice about any premarriage requirements. Each religion differs in its rules and restrictions, as do different branches within the same religion. Your first telephone conversation and meeting with the officiant should clear up most of the technical details and give you the opportunity to ask any questions you may have. After everything is settled, you can begin to create your ceremony with music, readings, special prayers, and personalized vows.

May other cultural and religious customs be included in the ceremony? What are the requirements to marry in the Roman Catholic, Protestant, or Jewish faiths?

Although religions differ too much to make a blanket statement about each one's requirements for marriage, the following should give you a general idea about what to expect:

❧ *Roman Catholic.* Couples must receive extensive Pre-Cana ("premarriage") counseling, involving discussions with your priest about your religious convictions and important marriage issues; workshops with other engaged couples; and compatibility quizzes. Marriage banns must be announced three times prior to the wedding date. If you've been married before in the Catholic Church, you must receive an annulment from the Church, which is a long and complicated procedure. See your priest for more information on this.

🙠 *Protestant.* Regardless of denomination, Protestant marriages have far fewer requirements and restrictions than Catholic marriages. One or more informal meetings with the minister is required. However, premarital counseling, though less rigorous than Pre-Cana, is common. You may also need to take compatibility quizzes. Sunday weddings are generally discouraged. There is no need for an annulment if either party has been divorced.

🙠 *Jewish.* The Orthodox and Conservative branches of Judaism have a few stipulations that are rigidly adhered to: Weddings may not take place on the Sabbath or during any other time that is considered holy, men must wear yarmulkes, and ceremonies are generally performed in Hebrew or Aramaic. Neither of these branches will conduct interfaith ceremonies, although some Reform rabbis will conduct interfaith ceremonies. Reform ceremonies are performed in both English and Hebrew. As in the Orthodox and Conservative traditions, however, Reform ceremonies cannot take place on the Sabbath or during holy times. If either party is divorced, the couple is required to obtain a Jewish divorce, or get, before they can marry. Preparations for the ceremony will differ, depending on the tradition. Check with your rabbi for specific details.

How do Roman Catholic, Protestant, and Jewish wedding ceremonies differ from one another?

Very briefly, the Roman Catholic wedding ceremony consists of Introductory Rites, including opening music selections, a greeting by the priest, and an opening prayer; Liturgy of the Word, including readings by your friends and family members, and a homily that focuses on some aspect of marriage; and the Rite of Marriage, including the declaration of consent and the exchange of vows and rings. Having a complete Mass is optional; with it, the ceremony will typically last 45 minutes.

The Protestant wedding ceremony varies somewhat among the denominations, but the basic elements are the same. The officiant welcomes the guests, and a Prayer of Blessing is said. Scripture passages are read, there is a Giving in Marriage (affirmation by parents), and the congregation gives its response. After vows and rings are exchanged, there is a celebration of the Lord's Supper, and the unity candle is lit, followed by the Benediction and recessional.

Judaism, too, has different "divisions" that adhere to different rules, but certain elements of the wedding ceremony are basically the same in the Orthodox, Conservative, and Reform traditions. The marriage ceremony is conducted under a chuppah, an ornamented canopy.

What are the requirements and characteristics of a Christian Science wedding?

Christian Science wedding ceremonies are very similar to Protestant ceremonies, except that the marriage must be performed by an ordained minister of the gospel or other proper legal authority. Also, and this is a big one, no alcohol can be served at the reception.

What are the requirements and characteristics of a Quaker wedding?

Given that the Quaker ethic is to reject worldly display, Quaker weddings are more Spartan than those of other faiths. A notice of intent to wed is read at least a month beforehand at a meeting of the Society of Friends. The ceremony itself may involve a procession, at the end of which the bride and groom take seats facing the congregation. They exchange vows and sign a marriage certificate.

What are the requirements and characteristics of an Eastern Orthodox wedding?

Unlike the Roman Catholic ceremony, the Eastern Orthodox (including Greek and Russian Orthodox) Church marriage is celebrated without a mass. Services are usually in the afternoon or in the evening. Although traditions are changing, the hour-long service takes place not at the altar but at a special table at the front of the church. The bride and groom hold lighted candles. Great importance is placed on the number three—to represent the Holy Trinity. Wedding rings are blessed, then exchanged three times. (Rings are worn on the right hand.) Crowns are placed on the couple's heads and switched back and forth three times. After the Gospel is read, the bride and groom take three sips each from a cup of wine. The congregation sings "God Grant Them Many Years," and the couple walks hand-in-hand around the ceremonial table three times.

Meeting with the Officiant

During the meeting with your officiant, be sure to get all the details concerning rules and restrictions, your church's feeling on interfaith marriages, required commitments to raise future children in your religion, and so on. Don't be afraid to ask any questions; you want to make sure that you and your church are on the same wavelength on these important issues. The following list should give you a good idea of what questions to ask, so don't leave home without it:

- Are the dates and times we're interested in available?
- What are the requirements for getting married in this church/synagogue?
- What are the premarital counseling requirements?
- Who will perform the ceremony? (You may be close to a particular officiant, only to find that he or she is not available at the time you want.)
- Are visiting clergy allowed to take part in the ceremony? If so, who will be responsible for what?
- What does the church or synagogue have available with regards to aisle runners, musical instruments, and musical talent? Is the church organ in good working order? What is the policy for bringing in our own organist (or other musicians)? Is there enough room at the site for additional singers and players?
- Are there any restrictions on decorations? On music?
- Will the wedding party be allowed into the ceremony site well in advance of the wedding to attend to decorations and setup?

Meeting with the Officiant *(continued)*

❧ Are any other weddings scheduled for the same day? If so, is there enough time between the two ceremonies to set up decorations and otherwise get things ready?

❧ Are there any restrictions on where the photographer and videographer may stand (or move) during the ceremony?

❧ Can friends and relatives take part in the ceremony as, say, readers or singers?

❧ Will we be allowed to hold the receiving line at the site—in the back of the church or synagogue, for instance, or in a courtyard? Is there enough room for this?

❧ What is the cost for the ceremony and the use of church or synagogue personnel and facilities? (This payment is typically referred to as a donation. It does not go to any single individual, but to the church or synagogue as a whole. These days, the suggested amount will range from $100 to $200.) The best man is traditionally responsible for giving the payment to the officiant at the ceremony's conclusion.

❧ How much parking is available?

❧ Will participation from another officiant be allowed (if yours will be an interfaith marriage)?

What are the requirements and characteristics of a Mormon wedding?

Only members of the Church of Jesus Christ of Latter-Day Saints who have received a Temple Recommend may attend a Mormon wedding ceremony. Non-Mormon friends of the bride and groom are invited to wait on the grounds of the temple and may join the newlyweds after the service.

What are the requirements and characteristics of a Muslim wedding?

Marriage is a contract, a covenant, under the Qur'an, and mutual assent, or affirmation, is required to make it binding. Under Islam, the bride's father presents the groom with a dowry, or *mahr*, commensurate with his means. It is paid half on the new wife's demand and the rest on the death of either party or the dissolution of the marriage, should that come to pass.

The marriage is publicly declared during Islamic services through a sermon or other announcement. After the ceremony there is a feast (*walimah*) celebrating the union.

What are the requirements and characteristics of a Hindu wedding?

Marriage (*vivaha*) is permitted between cousins, but not between castes. It is an essential practice for those who have not renounced the world.

The marriage of daughters is an expensive affair in which the bride's family gives gifts to the groom's family as part of her dowry. The father of the bride gives his gift to the father of the groom, and together they make an offering into a fire.

For the ceremony itself, the bride's wrist is tied with a small ribbon and she steps three times around a grinding stone belonging to the groom's family. The couple then takes seven steps around a sacred fire into which the groom makes an offering.

The ceremony and celebration may continue for several days before the bride begins to dwell in the groom's home.

What are the rules regarding interfaith marriages?

The Catholic church will sanction any marriage between a Catholic and non-Catholic providing that all of the Church's concerns are met. Contrary to popular belief, it is not necessary for, say, a Jewish person to convert to Catholicism in order to marry in a Catholic ceremony.

In marriages between a Protestant and a Catholic, officiants from both religions may take part in the ceremony if the couple wishes. However, in a Jewish-Christian wedding, even the most liberal clergy will not perform a joint ceremony in the temple or church. These ceremonies usually take place at the actual reception site.

What is a nondenominational wedding ceremony?

This is a spiritual ceremony without the structure and restrictions of traditional religions, typically resembling a traditional Protestant ceremony. It is offered by the Unitarian church or other nondenominational groups, which will perform interfaith marriages for nonmembers.

What is a military wedding?

If either you or your fiancé is in the military, you may want to consider having a military wedding. Military weddings are very formal affairs; they can look quite impressive, what with all of those uniformed guests and wedding party members. This type of wedding features what is perhaps the most visually stunning conclusion of them all: the newly married couple walks arm-in-arm from the altar beneath an archway of crossed swords!

A groom serving in the armed forces must wear his dress uniform in the ceremony. As part of his outfit he may wear a sword or saber, but never a boutonnière. If the groom does sport something with a long, sharp blade, the bride stands on his right, presumably to avoid shedding blood on that nice white dress. If he doesn't wear a sword, she stands on the left.

A military bride has the choice of wearing her dress uniform or a traditional wedding gown. Other military personnel in the wedding party, male or female, usually wear military garb.

As if doing a seating plan for a regular wedding weren't stressful enough, the seating at a military wedding has to account for high-ranking officers and special officials. These people must be seated in places of honor. The remainder of the military guests should be seated by rank. And if you thought you'd seen enough of swords at the ceremony, you're not through yet; tradition dictates that the bride and groom cut the first piece of their wedding cake with a sword.

Despite the differences in attire and protocol, as well as the extensive use of weaponry, a military wedding can nonetheless be as much like a traditional wedding as you wish.

Can a civil ceremony have all the trimmings of a traditional church wedding?

Yes. Contrary to the stereotype of a barren scene in a judge's chambers that takes all of 20 seconds, being "civil" does not necessarily mean being boring, quick, or small. Rent a hotel ballroom, a public garden, a yacht, or some other exotic locale for the ceremony and reception. Granted, it won't be a religious setting, and religious officials will not be present, but you can still summon up a scene of power and drama.

What are the legal requirements for a civil ceremony?

You should contact your city hall for information. Generally, a county clerk, judge, magistrate, or justice of the peace can perform legally binding ceremonies. You must first obtain a marriage license, and you'll need two witnesses. Most civil ceremonies take place in a courthouse or government office; if the officiant must travel to perform your ceremony, you should invite him or her to the reception.

Must all religious weddings take place in a house of worship?

No. Jewish weddings may also take place at the reception location: a hotel ballroom, function hall, country club, or the locale of your choice. Catholics and Protestants usually discourage having religious weddings outside the church. Again, check with your officiant for details.

My church won't allow flash photography in the sanctuary. How can I let guests know of this?

Flash photography can be disconcerting during a wedding ceremony, and many churches and synagogues forbid it. If you're printing up a wedding program, include that information inside. Otherwise, post a sign outside the sanctuary alerting guests to this fact.

What is "jumping the broom"?

Jumping the broom is an African-American tradition that many couples are now incorporating into the marriage ceremony. The custom began in the United States during the 1600s. Since marriage between slaves was illegal, men and women would jump over a broom, which symbolized homemaking, and were then considered married. Again, if you're having a religious ceremony, check with your officiant to make sure this will be allowed.

Wedding Customs International

If you've noticed that notions of etiquette vary from region to region, imagine the discrepancies to be found from country to country. As you struggle to remain an upstanding and proper bride-to-be, take a break to mull over some of these, shall we say, more exotic wedding traditions. If any should strike your fancy, you might choose to include them and spice up your wedding day.

Africa

Though many women might not consider the sentiment well wishing, the common greeting to a new bride in some tribes is, "May thou bear 12 children with him." Some African ceremonies include the binding of the couples' wrists with plaited grass.

Belgium

The bride takes a family handkerchief with her name newly embroidered on it with her to the wedding. After the ceremony, it is framed and displayed in the family house until another daughter gets married; then she carries it and adds her name.

Bermuda

The new husband and wife plant a tree to symbolize their love and union.

What's It All Mean?

The Chuppah (or the Jewish Wedding Canopy) –
The Jewish wedding ceremony takes place under a
wedding canopy, the *chuppah*. Among other things,
the chuppah symbolizes the new home that will be
created by the couple. In ancient times it was a spe-
cially decorated tent that had been set up in the courtyard of the bride's family home. Back then, the
newlyweds actually lived there for seven days of
feasting after the wedding.

Over the years, the chuppah evolved into a
canopy supported by four poles, which were often decorated with garlands of flowers and greenery. Note: If
you decide to use flowers check with the rabbi to be
sure it will be acceptable. Some synagogues do not
allow a floral canopy. This canopy is optional in the
Reform ceremony. The Seven Blessings are recited.
After the bride and groom drink blessed wine, the
groom smashes a glass with his foot, symbolizing the
destruction of the temple of Jerusalem and fragility of
life. Then the newly married couple is toasted with a
cheer of "Mazel tov!" ("Good luck!")

Czech Republic

The bride wears a wreath made of rosemary to symbolize love, loyalty, and wisdom.

China

In the Chinese wedding ceremony, a goblet of honey and a goblet of wine are tied together with a red ribbon. Red is the color of love, the ribbon stands for unity. The bride and groom take a drink to symbolize a union of love. After a wedding dinner that might feature delicacies like bear nose, the guests receive fortune cookies for good luck.

Egypt

For the rowdiest wedding procession you're likely to see, head to Egypt. Belly dancers, men brandishing swords, and people blowing loud horns all accompany the wedding party and guests as they troop from the ceremony to the reception. In an interesting twist, the guests wear traditional Egyptian clothing, but the bride dresses in a Western-style wedding gown.

England

In the English countryside, the bride and her attendants walk to the church on a floor strewn with flower petals, meant to guarantee a smooth and joyous path through life. As the couple enters the church, the bells chime; when they exit as husband and wife, they chime again, only to a different tune. (Bells were once believed to ward off evil spirits.)

Finland

In days gone by, the bride-to-be was crowned with gold during the ceremony. Afterwards, she was blindfolded and surrounded by all of the unmarried female guests.

The bride groped around blindly until she picked someone to pass the crown to. The one the bride crowned was believed to be the next to wed (much like the bouquet-catcher).

France

Couples drink a toast from a "coupe de marriage," a two-handled silver cup. The cup is passed down through the family to future couples. For a refreshing change, the guests bring the flowers to the reception to help the couple celebrate life and their new beginning. (Considering how big your florist's bill can be, you'll probably wish this idea would catch on here.)

Germany

In another tradition that some American women might like to see catch on in the United States, both the bride and the groom wear gold bands as a symbol of their engagement. A custom not too many American women are likely to be fond of, however, is the one that encourages the groom to kneel on the hem of the bride's dress during the ceremony, as a sign that he is now her boss. The bride sets him straight by getting up and stepping on his foot.

Greece

During the ceremony, the bride and groom wear crowns made from flowers, signifying their entrance into marriage. The couple takes three sips of wine and walks around the altar three times with the priest, which symbolizes the Trinity. The groom's Godfather (or another honored male family member, known as *koumbaros*) has an important part in the ceremony: he is the one who crowns the couple.

Holland

An awning or canopy of sorts made of evergreen is set up for the couple; they sit under it on thrones during a prewedding party given by the families. The evergreens are meant to symbolize everlasting love. As the couple "holds court," the party guests approach them to wish them luck and happiness.

India

The families of both the bride and groom prepare puffed rice for the ceremony as a symbol of fertility and good luck. The groom's brother douses the new husband and wife with flower petals at the ceremony's end. Henna dye is used to paint designs on the couple's hands; the couple usually leaves their handprints on the outside door of their new home for good luck.

Ireland

Many Irish believe there is a lucky day for weddings, one that comes but once a year: New Year's Day. For good luck, a swatch of Irish lace may be sewn into the bride's gown; the couple also receives a horseshoe to put up in their new home. Although they are now popular in America simply as friendship rings, Claddagh rings remain the standard Irish wedding ring. The heart, crown, and hands found on the Claddagh symbolize love, loyalty, and friendship.

Italy

The lucky villagers are recipients of cakes and other baked goodies passed out by the bride and groom as they wind their way through the streets. For the departing couple, there are no clanging cans on the back of the car; instead, the front grill is decorated with flowers to symbolize the road to a happy marriage.

Japan

The Japanese hold the distinction of putting on some of the most extravagant wedding ceremonies in the Eastern world. Part of the Japanese wedding ceremony requires both the bride and groom to take nine sips of sake. They may be a little tipsy after the nine sips, but they are considered married after the first. During the ceremony, the bride will leave to change clothes three to four times. (And you thought finding one wedding gown was tough!) As usual, the groom has it easy, wearing only one black kimono. Guests at a Japanese wedding are very lucky—not only are they fed and entertained, but the wedding favors they receive from the couple's families sometimes add up to half the price of the gifts given to the couple.

Lithuania

The parents of the bride and groom give them gifts that stand for the elements of marriage: wine for joy, salt for tears, and bread for work.

Mexico

The couple is joined by a white silk cord wrapped around their shoulders to signify their union in marriage. In some ceremonies, the silk cord is replaced by a large string of rosary beads, wrapped around the couple in the form of a figure eight. After the ceremony, the couple dances in a heart-shaped circle formed by the guests.

Philippines

Here, they also use the white silk cord. Unlike the United States, the groom's family pays for the wedding; they also give the bride old coins which stand for prosperity. In return, the bride's family gives the new couple a cash dowry.

Poland

For the privilege of dancing with the bride, guests put money into the pockets of an apron she wears over her wedding dress. The money collected from "Dollar Dance" is supposed to go toward paying for the honeymoon. (Imagine how many such dances it would take for a trip to Hawaii—then again, it's a step up from the ten-cents-a-dance craze of yesteryear.)

Romania

If you have a feeling you may be a hungry bride, Romania is the place to marry; there guests shower the newlyweds with nuts and candy, meant to symbolize prosperity.

Russia

Oh, to be a guest here! In some parts of Russia, rather than bring a gift to the wedding, all non-family-member guests receive a gift.

Spain

The bride embroiders a shirt for the groom, which he wears on their wedding day; she herself wears orange blossoms and a mantilla. In an unusual turn, the bride and groom wear their wedding bands on their right hands.

Sweden

No matter how stressed or frazzled, the couple is sure to smell very nice in Sweden. The bride carries a bouquet of herbs in hopes that the fragrance will ward off trolls; the groom's attire comes complete with some thyme sewn in. In an era of pumps and high-heels, one Swedish tradition is no longer popular, but in days of old, the bride kept her shoes untied for the entire wedding day. (In case you're wondering, yes, she would even consummate the marriage with her shoes on!) If, in the course of her night's sleep, the shoes would slip off, it was a sign that she would bear children easily. (The idea apparently being that kids will slip out as easily as the shoes slip off.)

Switzerland

Junior bridesmaids begin the wedding procession by throwing colored handkerchiefs to the guests. Those who catch a hanky are supposed to give money to help the couple start out. (Lucky them!)

United States

In the early days of the country, guests did not give appliances or money to the couple—they provided the newly-weds with some stamina-giving sack posset, a drink consisting of hot spiced milk and brew.

Before the Civil War, African-American brides believed that the best days to get married were Tuesdays and Wednesdays because that would ensure a long and happy life with one's husband.

Wales

The bride's attendants receive a gift of myrtle from the bride; the flower's blooming is said to predict another wedding.

CHAPTER NINE

Behind the Scenes: Planning Your Ceremony

*L*ike many couples, you and your fiancé may be looking for something different to say and do at the altar, an alternative to the traditional wedding ceremony. If you decide to personalize your ceremony, start by considering what is important to both of you. You're in charge—so customize the proceedings to your own values and dreams. Though most religions allow some flexibility in their ceremonies these days, be sure to check with your officiant about rules and guidelines. Here are some areas that couples often personalize:

- Readings. Your officiant will provide you with a list of recommended readings, most of which focus on some aspect of togetherness and marriage. If you have a favorite passage you'd like to read, ask your officiant if it would be possible to include it in the ceremony.
- Music. As with the readings, you will have a broad range of choices here. Most officiants request that the songs you select be religious in nature, but that doesn't mean you're restricted to music you'll hear only in a church. If you can find commercially released songs that meet the proper criteria, you will most likely be able to include them on your play list.
- Vows. If you feel comfortable baring your soul before a roomful of people, you may want to write your own vows. If you don't feel quite comfortable with that, but still find the traditional vows lacking somehow, perhaps there is a poem or passage that expresses your feelings. Before you break out your pad and pen to write the ultimate love sonnet, though, let your officiant know about your intentions. Some religions can be strict about what vows must be said, while others are willing to bend a little.

🍃 Symbolic ceremonies. Include a wine ceremony or a ceremony for the lighting of the unity candle. As you walk up the aisle, give a single flower from your bouquet to your mother and your groom's mother. Take your vows by candlelight, and have the church bells rung immediately as you are declared husband and wife. Be sure to consult with your officiant first about any restrictions. Be creative!

Ceremony Seating

Which side of the church is appropriate for the bride's family?

Although it's not mandatory, the bride's family usually sits on the left side of the church for a Christian ceremony, while the groom's family sits on the right. The reverse is true for Reform and Conservative Jewish weddings. If one side has many more guests than the other, you may dispense with this custom and sit everyone together to achieve a more balanced look. However, men and women are usually segregated in Orthodox Jewish ceremonies.

My fiancé and I are writing our own wedding vows. We've come up with one paragraph that says it all; our other one isn't quite so great. How do we decide who gets to say the perfect vow?

Instead of playing rock, paper, scissors to decide who has to say the lesser vow, consider the possibility that both of you can recite the same perfect paragraph. Reciting the same vow will symbolize unity of purpose and the spirit of cooperation within your marriage. And if you think about it, this is how the church has been doing it for years.

I recently received a wedding invitation that specified "in the ribbons." What does this mean?

In some ceremonies, the first few rows of pews or chairs are sectioned off by ribbons, meaning they are reserved for family and very special friends.

My parents are divorced. Where should they be seated during the ceremony?

Typically, parents are seated in the first row (or in the second if the attendants will be seated during the ceremony). In the case of divorce, the bride's natural mother has the privilege of sitting in the first row, and of selecting those who will sit with her, including her spouse if she has remarried. If your divorced parents have remained amicable, your father may sit in the second row with his spouse or significant other. If there is some acrimony between the two parties, however, your father should be seated a few rows farther back. However, if you have been raised by your stepmother and prefer to give her the honor, she and your father may sit in the first row, while your mother sits farther back.

Where should my siblings and grandparents be seated during the ceremony?

Your siblings should sit in the second row, behind your mother and father. Grandparents sit in the third row, and close friends and relatives sit in the fourth.

In what order should everyone be seated?

Guests are seated as they arrive, from front to back. The mothers of the bride and groom should be seated just before the ceremony begins. Late-arriving guests are not escorted to their seats by ushers. They should take seats near the back of the church, preferably via a side aisle.

The Processional

In what order do attendants walk down the aisle in Christian ceremonies?

In a Catholic processional, the bridesmaids walk down the aisle, one by one, while the ushers and best man wait at the altar. Who goes first is usually determined by height, from shortest to tallest. For large weddings with more than four bridesmaids, they walk in pairs. The honor attendant is next, followed by the ring bearer and flower girl. The bride then enters on her father's right arm, followed by pages (if any), who carry the bride's train. The Protestant processional is the same, except ushers may precede the bridesmaids in pairs, according to height.

In what order do attendants walk down the aisle in Jewish ceremonies?

Orthodox, Conservative, and Reform processions vary according to the families' preferences, devoutness, and local custom. A traditional religious Jewish processional may begin with the rabbi and cantor (with the cantor on the rabbi's right), followed by the ushers walking one by one, and the best man. The groom then walks between his mother (on his right) and his father (on his left). The bridesmaids then walk one by one, followed by the maid of honor, the page, and the flower girl. The bride is the last to enter, with her mother on her right and her father on her left.

My church has two side aisles instead of a single center aisle. Which aisle should we use for the processional?

In this case, your officiant will most likely advise you to use the left aisle for the processional and the right aisle for the recessional.

Suggested Music

Here is a compilation of selections, that have proven
popular for various parts of the wedding ceremony.

The Processional:

This is the music that accompanies the wedding
party in their jaunt down the aisle. A traditional
march helps to set the pace for nervous feet—and
carry the spirit of the day toward the altar. When it's
time for you to make that long trek down the aisle,
you can walk to the same piece as the bridesmaids,
or to a piece chosen especially for you. Oftentimes
the bride will walk to the same song as the bridesmaids, but played at a different tempo. Some processional favorites (and their composers) include:

"Waltz of the Flowers," Tchaikovsky
"Wedding March," Mendelssohn
Bridal Chorus ("Here Comes the Bride"), Wagner
"Trumpet Voluntary," Dupuis
"Trumpet Voluntary," Clarke
"Trumpet Tune," Purcell
"The Dance of the Sugar Plum Fairies," Tchaikovsky
"Ode to Joy," Beethoven
"The March," Tchaikovsky
"Ave Maria," Schubert
"The Austrian Wedding March," traditional

The Ceremony:

Music played while the wedding ceremony itself
takes place is called, oddly enough, ceremony music.
The right music here can enhance the mood and
emphasize the meaning of the marriage ceremony.

Suggested Music *(continued)*

Some ceremony music favorites (and their composers) include:

"My Tribute," Crouch
"The Lord's Prayer," Malotte
"Panis Angelicus," Franck
"Now Thank We All Our God," Bach
"Saviour Like a Shepherd Lead Us," Bradbury
"Cherish the Treasure," Mohr
"We've Only Just Begun," The Carpenters
"The Unity Candle Song," Sullivan
"The Bride's Prayer," Good
"The Wedding Prayer," Dunlap
"All I Ask of You," Norbet and Callahan
"Wherever You Go," Callahan
"The Wedding Song," Paul Stookey
"The Irish Wedding Song," traditional

The Recessional:

This is your exit music. The song should be joyous and upbeat, reflecting your happiness at being joined for life to the man accompanying you back down the aisle. Some recessional favorites (and their composers) include:

"The Russian Dance," Tchaikovsky
"Trumpet Tune," Stanley
"Toccata Symphony V," Widor
"All Creatures of Our God and King," Williams
"Trumpet Fanfare (Rondeau)," Mouret
"Pomp and Circumstance," Elgar
"Praise, My Soul, the King of Heaven," Goss

My father has passed away. Who should escort me down the aisle?

There is really no single answer; do whatever feels most comfortable to you. If your mother has remarried and you are close to your stepfather, he may be a good choice. Otherwise, a brother, a grandfather, a special uncle, or a close family friend could also do the honors. Some brides walk down the aisle with their mother or with their groom. Others choose to walk without an escort. Keep in mind that whomever you choose will sit in the front pew with your mother during the ceremony (except if you choose your groom, of course).

My parents are divorced and my mother has remarried. Is it more appropriate for my father or my stepfather to walk me down the aisle?

Again, this really depends on your preference and family situation. To avoid risking a civil war, however, you should take care to somehow include both men in the proceedings. If you've remained close to your father, you may prefer that he fulfill his traditional role, while your stepfather does a reading. Or they may both escort you down the aisle. Often in Jewish ceremonies, divorced parents both walk the bride down the aisle.

This is my second marriage. Who should walk me down the aisle?

Many second-time brides walk down the aisle with their grooms, or with one of their children. It's also appropriate for your father to escort you again, or for you to walk alone.

I'd like to drop the outdated tradition of the father giving the bride away. Are there any alternatives?

Yes, there are several traditions more in keeping with the times, which you should discuss with your officiant.

Instead of asking "Who gives this woman . . . ?" he or she may ask, "Who blesses this union?" Your father may respond, "Her mother and I do," and take his seat next to your mother. It is also entirely appropriate for both parents to respond, "We do." In this case, your mother should stand up when the officiant asks, "Who blesses this union?"

In a double wedding, do the brides walk down the aisle together? If not, how do we decide who goes first?

This question touches on the most important piece of protocol in a double wedding. The undisputed law of etiquette is clear: The older of the two brides is the first to perform all key wedding rites, and so she is the one who proceeds down the aisle first with her wedding party. As you might imagine, two full wedding parties can get rather large, so find a place that can accommodate everyone. However, aside from the fact that everything is done twice, the double wedding can be just like any other wedding.

What role do grandparents play in a wedding?

Your grandmother wears a corsage that coordinates with the colors of the bridal party and sits in the third pew with your grandfather. The groom's grandmother also wears a coordinating corsage and sits in the third pew with her husband. In some formal Jewish weddings, grandparents are included in the processional. At the reception, they'll either sit with your parents or at their own table with other family members.

The Recessional

What is the appropriate order of the recessional?

Arm in arm, you and your new husband (yes, your husband!) lead the recessional, followed by your child attendants. Your maid of honor and best man are next, followed by your bridesmaids, who are paired with ushers. The order of the Jewish recession is as follows: bride and groom, bride's parents, groom's parents, child attendants, honor attendants, and bridesmaids paired with ushers. The cantor and rabbi walk at the end of the recession.

When do we sign the marriage license?

After the recessional, you, your groom, and your honor attendants will join the officiant in his or her chambers or at a side altar to "make it official."

When should we pay the officiant?

The best man typically gives the officiant his or her fee in a discreet envelope, provided by the groom or his family, when the bride and groom sign the marriage license.

 ## What's It All Mean?

Giving the Bride Away

Back when a daughter was considered her father's possession, some formal transfer was necessary during the wedding ritual. (At one time, old shoes—themselves a symbol of ownership and power over a woman—were actually thrown at the bride by her father to symbolize his yielding possession of her to the groom!) Today, the custom symbolizes the parents' acceptance of the bride's passage from child to adult, and a sign of their blessing of her marriage to her chosen groom.

CHAPTER TEN

Places, Please:
The Rehearsal Dinner

*A*t some point before the wedding, usually the night before, all interested parties, including the bride, groom, bridesmaids, ushers, officiant, parents, and readers gather at the ceremony site and do a quick run-through of the ceremony. Basically, the officiant tells everybody where to stand, what to do, and when to do it. Ushers learn all their duties, readers practice their readings, and soloists run through their pieces. After everyone understands what they're supposed to do, the whole gang leaves and goes to dinner.

Who's supposed to pay for the rehearsal dinner?

The groom's family traditionally pays for the rehearsal dinner as a way to thank the bride's parents for their generosity in hosting the wedding. But today, anybody (for example, the bride's parents or grandparents) can host the dinner (see Chapter Two for a traditional breakdown of costs).

Do we need to send out invitations for the rehearsal dinner?

No. Written invitations are optional for this event, since the rehearsal dinner is usually small and informal. Usually a simple phone call to all guests will suffice for this occasion. But if formal invitations are issued, they should be sent by the host or hosts of the dinner.

We're on a limited budget. How formal does the rehearsal dinner have to be?

The rehearsal dinner is supposed to be an informal event designed so that the bride and groom can relax with family and friends on the night before their big day. No dress code, invitations, or etiquette rules need apply. The event can be anything from a pizza party at the groom's parents' house to a sit-down dinner at a restaurant or club. Just make sure that the rehearsal is not so lavish that it eclipses the reception.

My fiancé's mother thinks she doesn't need to pay for our guests' drinks at the rehearsal dinner. Is she right?

No! A rehearsal dinner should be a relatively small gathering of those friends and relatives closest to the bride and groom; these guests shouldn't be expected to pay for anything.

Who should go to the rehearsal dinner?

Anyone who has a part in the wedding should go to the dinner, including both sets of parents, your immediate families, attendants and their significant others, any child attendants and their parents, and the officiant and his or her spouse.

Does anyone else need to be invited to the dinner?

Most couples also invite their grandparents, siblings and their significant others, and other close relatives to the rehearsal dinner. If you'd like, you may also invite other hired hands, such as the organist, the soloists, and their spouses.

I've heard of people inviting out-of-town guests to the rehearsal dinner. Is this necessary?

It's not required, but if it's within your budget, asking out-of-town guests to your rehearsal dinner is certainly a nice gesture.

Who should make a toast?

Although no rule states that you must make toasts at the rehearsal dinner, traditionally the best man is the first to toast the couple. This toast is usually more lighthearted than the one he makes at the reception. Then the groom can toast his bride and future in-laws, and the bride can toast her groom and future in-laws. Sometimes the couple's parents like to get in a few words as well. Feel free to have as many toasts as you'd like; if everyone wants to make a toast and the mood calls for it, let them! Try to have these toasts in the intimacy of the rehearsal dinner, rather than at the reception.

Is this the right time to give attendants their gifts?

Many couples choose the rehearsal dinner as the time to give gifts to the wedding party. The gifts are just a small thank-you for all the work and money your wedding party has put into the wedding. It's common to give all the bridesmaids or groomsmen the same gift. Of course, you can always individualize a little bit. Bridesmaids usually get some accessory (earrings, necklace, or stockings) that they can wear on the wedding day; ushers can get shaving kits, cologne, or silk ties. It's also nice for you and your fiancé to get gifts for your parents. After all, in many cases, they've put a lot of time and money into your big day.

 Wording the Rehearsal Dinner Invitations

If you're thinking about sending out invites for the rehearsal dinner, here is a sample you may wish to follow:

Mr. and Mrs. (Hosts)
request your company
at a rehearsal dinner
on the eve of the marriage of
**Samantha Jennifer Cook and
Andrew Nathaniel Wilkinson**
at Morton's Steak House
on Friday, the sixteenth of June
123 West Grand Avenue
Chicago, Illinois

CHAPTER ELEVEN

We're Having a Party: Planning Your Reception

*U*nless you and your fiancé decided to elope as soon as someone mentioned the words "guest list," you're probably planning a reception for after the ceremony. And unless you're simply going to serve cake and punch in your parents' backyard, the reception will undoubtedly give you more fits and headaches than any other aspect of your wedding. To ensure that the biggest party of your life will go off without a hitch, you have to coordinate flowers, music, food, wine, cakes, dances, and photographers, all within a budget that won't force your parents to declare bankruptcy.

My maid of honor told me I should look for a reception site, and then choose my wedding date depending upon what's available. Shouldn't I choose my date first, and then find a reception site?

Your way might be more traditional, but practically speaking, your maid of honor is right. Once you know when you'd like to get married—in the spring or fall, for instance—it's easier to choose a reception site and church and then pick out a specific date based upon the site's availability. Reception sites are often booked a year in advance, especially for dates during the peak wedding months of April through October. So unless you and your fiancé would like to get married on a specific day, such as the anniversary of your first date, it's best to just pick a day when both your church and reception site are available.

Our reception won't start until two hours after the ceremony. Am I responsible for my guests in the interim?

Yes! If a delay is inevitable, you should make sure that your guests, especially those from out of town, will be entertained between the ceremony and reception. Set up a hospitality suite at a nearby hotel, or ask a close friend to have cocktails or hors d'oeuvres at his or her house. If the reason for the delay is that you're planning on having photographs taken during that time, you might also consider taking them before the ceremony or at the reception.

Eat, Drink, and Be Merry

Many brides feel pressured to have a large, formal reception because they think their guests will expect it. But that's really unnecessary. As long as you provide refreshments for your guests, it doesn't matter what form the reception takes—it can be anything from an informal cocktail hour to an elegant, catered brunch. You don't have to break the bank in order to have an unforgettable reception.

Our reception will begin at one o'clock and be over by five o'clock. Do we need to serve a sit-down meal, or can we just serve hors d'oeuvres?

There's no rule that says you must serve a five-course meal at your reception. As long as your reception doesn't fall during a typical mealtime, finger sandwiches or hors d'oeuvres would be absolutely appropriate. But if your reception will take place from five through nine o'clock, you must serve a full meal, since your guests will be expecting it.

We want to offer a choice of entrees at our reception. How can we find out what our guests want?

While it's not traditional, offering your guests a choice of entrees is quite thoughtful. The easiest way to find out is to write the choices (for example, chicken or beef) on the response card, and let your guests circle their choice. This way, you'll know exactly how many Beef Wellingtons and Chicken Kievs to order.

What to Ask the Reception Site Manager

With all the wonderful reception options open to you, you'll have to narrow down your list and start to evaluate the individual sites. Since the reception is probably going to be the most expensive part of your wedding, it's important to take the proper steps from the start to get every penny's worth. Here are some questions you should ask:

- How many people can the facility comfortably seat? How big is the dance floor?
- Is an in-house catering service offered? If it is, and if you don't wish to use it, can you bring in your own caterer?
- Are tables, chairs, dinnerware, and linens supplied? What about decorations?
- Is the site an appropriate one for live music? Is there proper spacing, wiring, and equipment?
- Does the site coordinator have any recommendations for setup and decorations? Are there any florists, bands, or disc jockeys he or she can recommend?
- Can you see photos of previous reception setups?
- How many hours is the site available for? Is there a time minimum you must meet? Are there charges if the reception runs overtime?
- Is there free parking? If there is valet parking, what are the rates and gratuities? (If you pay for valet parking up front, post a sign informing your guests that the tip has already been paid.)
- Will there be coatroom and restroom attendants? A bartender? A doorman? What are the charges for these?

What to Ask the Reception Site Manager *(continued)*

🔔 If you've arranged for an open bar, do you have to bring the alcohol or does the site provide it?

🔔 If you've arranged for a cash bar, what will the prices be?

🔔 Does the facility have more than one reception site on the premises? If someone else is occupying another room at the site, will there still be adequate parking available? Is there enough space between the two rooms to ensure privacy? (You don't want your jazz quartet drowned out by the heavy metal band playing at the graduation party next door.)

🔔 Will the site coordinator be available to advise you on decorations? Layout? Seating?

🔔 Is there a separate room where photographs can be taken? Where can you change into your going-away clothes?

🔔 Who pays for any police or security that may be required? (It is customary for a policeman to be present at public function sites where alcohol is being served.)

🔔 What is the layout of the tables? How many people can sit comfortably at each table?

🔔 Are the costs (room rental, catering, etc.) fixed? If not, what is the ceiling for each cost?

🔔 Will your deposit be returned in the event of a cancellation?

🔔 Are there any other possible reception-related charges?

If we're having a buffet at our reception, is it inappropriate for the wedding party to be served at their seats?

No guest really expects the bride to stand in the buffet line in her wedding gown, so it's perfectly acceptable for everybody at the head table to get plated service. Just make sure your caterer can provide both plated and buffet service.

Should we provide meals for the band and photographer?

You don't need to feed them the same $40 Beef Wellington that your guests are eating, but you should have some sort of nourishment, like snacks or sandwiches, available for them. Many professionals put a clause in their contract that calls for a full meal, so examine your contract carefully.

Is it necessary to serve dessert in addition to the wedding cake?

No. It's perfectly appropriate to serve your cake as dessert. Of course, if you'd like to serve an additional dessert with your wedding cake, there's nothing wrong with that either.

I'm on a tight budget. I know that I have the option to set up a cash bar instead of an open bar, but I would feel guilty asking my guests to pay for their drinks. What should I do?

Fortunately, there are a few things you can do to allay your guilt. Have an open bar only for the first hour of the reception. This will get things off on the right foot and ease your guilty conscience.

Another option is to offer tray service; your guests won't have to pay for their drinks and you won't have to incur the massive expense of an open bar. Tray service can be accomplished by choosing a few drinks that you feel will be popular with the majority of your guests (include beer and wine for sure bets). The waitstaff will pass these selections around on a tray, offering them to your guests. The servers do not float around with drinks all night, but serve them on a schedule to keep down costs (and, of course, overconsumption). You might want to send the servers around before dinner, as dinner is being served, and at other appropriate times during the reception. It's wise to stop serving well before the end of the reception to give people a chance to sober up. Obviously, tray service will cost you more than a cash bar, but at least

What to Eat and When

Please keep in mind that the following guidelines are just that. You can be creative if you wish. It's unlikely you would want to schedule a luncheon reception at 7:00 at night, but if you want a sit down dinner at 2:00, go ahead and serve one. Just make sure to apprise all of the guests of the kind of reception you are planning. For instance, if you schedule a cocktail reception for 7:30, many guests will assume that you will be serving dinner, unless told otherwise. So specify all the details on the invitation.

Luncheon wedding: Between 12:00 and 2:00
Tea reception: Between 2:00 and 4:00
Cocktail reception: Between 4:00 and 7:30
Dinner reception: Between 7:00 and 9:00

you can regulate how much liquor gets consumed without offending your guests.

Serving a free champagne punch is also something to consider. A punch like this is fairly light, alcohol-wise, and people just aren't likely to pound down glass after glass. Maybe it's an image thing.

Or, you can rack up the savings by placing bottles of wine on tables. A typical bottle of wine holds four to five glasses. At a table seated for eight, a bottle of red and a bottle of white ensures that everyone gets a glass or two with their meal. You control the expense and consumption by purchasing a set number of bottles, and your guests get a free glass of wine to raise in your honor.

Finally, you can opt to serve beer and wine only. If your reception site allows it, you may be able to save some of your parents' hard-earned money by purchasing a few kegs or several cases of high-quality beer, plus some cases of good wine. Guests would be able to drink either on the house; all other types of alcohol could be made available at a cash bar.

My fiancé's father is an alcoholic. Should we avoid serving drinks at the reception?

That depends. Have your fiancé talk to his father about it. If his father is comfortable around alcohol and will not feel tempted to drink, go ahead and serve drinks. If your fiancé isn't sure his father will be able to stay on the wagon and would feel more comfortable if liquor wasn't served, there are plenty of festive nonalcoholic alternatives you could offer. Naturally, you should also consult your parents, or whoever is hosting the wedding as well.

A few of my friends have been known to experiment with recreational drugs. But I don't want them doing drugs at my wedding. What should I do?

If you suspect that some friends or relatives may want to consume substances that get them happy but can also get them arrested (read: illegal drugs), taking steps to ensure that it won't happen at your wedding is well within your rights. You don't want your big day tarnished by drugs or trouble with the law. Tell your friends in advance: no drugs whatsoever, not even in a quiet stall in the restroom. At the very least, it may offend other guests. At the very worst, it may provide you with the kind of "memorable wedding event" everyone would rather forget.

We're having a luncheon reception. Can we serve alcohol that early?

Liquor can be served anytime, from mimosas at brunch to a full-scale open bar at a nighttime reception. For a luncheon reception, a fully stocked bar is unnecessary—mimosas, champagne, bloody marys, or other light drinks would be more appropriate.

Grilling the Caterer

No matter what type of caterer you need, there are a number of key questions you should ask before making a commitment. Once you've found a caterer with all the right answers, make sure to get every part of your agreement in writing.

💐 What is the final food price? Caterers usually quote you an estimated price based on food prices at that time. About 90 days before the wedding (or perhaps later), they should give you the final price, reflecting current food rates. Early on, ask for an estimate of how much the price will change between the estimated figure and the actual cost. (You don't want to be charged $30 per meal if the estimate was $18.) Ask about price guarantees.

- ✿ What types of meal service are offered? Sit-down? Buffet? Stations? Russian? Sit-down and buffet are the most common, but at an extremely formal affair you might want Russian-style service where the food is brought out on large platters by trained waiters. The waiters either serve each person from the platter or guests serve themselves. No matter how simple or fancy the service, if you want it, you'd better make sure your caterer can deliver.

- ✿ Are there several meal options? Do they specialize in any particular cuisine?

- ✿ Is the catering service covered? If you are counting on them to provide liquor, do they have liability insurance to cover accidents that could occur after the wedding as a result of drunk driving? (It should go without saying that the caterer must have a liquor license if liquor will be served by staff!)

- ✿ What will the ratio of staff to guests be? Will there be enough people to man the tables? Will those people be dressed appropriately for the occasion?

- ✿ Will they make provisions for guests with special dietary needs? It's only proper that you plan ahead for guests on vegetarian, low-cholesterol, or kosher diets.

- ✿ Will meals be provided for the disc jockey (or band), photographer, and videographer? They get hungry, too.

- ✿ Does the caterer offer hors d'oeuvres? At what cost? What is the price difference between having them served by waiters and waitresses and dis-playing them on a buffet table?

- ✿ Can the caterer provide a wedding cake? How about a sweet table (with lots of cavity-causing, artery-clogging and blood-sugar-surging desserts)? At what price?

- Is there a "cake-cutting fee"? Some caterers won't bat an eyelash at hitting you with this charge (often as high as $3 per person), which supposedly goes to cover the labor cost of slicing the cake, plus forks and plates. *It is an outrageous idea!* You are already paying mandatory labor and gratuities fees for the staff. Do your very best to negotiate your way out of this ridiculous cost.

- Can you inspect linens, dinnerware, and related items? You don't want brown tablecloths unless you ask for them.
- Does the caterer's fee include gratuities for the staff, or will you be hit with that bill later? What about the cost of coat room attendants, bartenders, and others who may be working at the reception?
- What is the refund policy, in the unlikely event you should have to cancel? Better safe than sorry.
- What does the caterer do with leftover food? Since you're paying for it, you may wish to have it boxed up for yourself—or perhaps given to the local charity.
- If you are not familiar with a caterer's work, ask for references.

Variations on a Theme

While some people would question the propriety of a theme wedding, the fact is that although these types of affairs are indeed a step away from the traditional, they do have a way of making weddings considerably more special, both to the couple and to the guests. Depending on the theme you choose, you can live out your fantasies of living in another time or another place—or in a whole new way. Here are some ideas. (*Note:* Be sure to share whatever theme idea you have with your guests so they can dress appropriately.)

A Period Piece

The period wedding theme emphasizes the traditions, costumes, music, and customs of an earlier time period. Though the 1920s through the 1960s are the most popular periods, you could opt for Colonial America or Victorian England if you prefer—as long as you can find the costumes.

An Ethnic Flare

There's no better way to say "I'm proud of my heritage" than to orchestrate an ethnic-themed wedding. If you and your fiancé would like to highlight the culture and costumes of your ethnic background, this right here is the theme for you.

A Western Bonanza

Cowboy hats abound at these Western-style weddings. But that's only the tip of the pioneer spirit; also on the menu are fiddles, square dancing, horses, barbecue fare, and anything else that's associated with the wild frontier.

A Happy Holiday

A wedding set during a holiday season can take advantage of the decorations and spirit of that time. Valentine's Day, with its emphasis on love and romance, is a popular wedding time; Christmas is right up there, too. Easter and Passover are less popular because of certain religious restrictions, but a patriotic motif, complete with fireworks, might be a great idea for the Fourth of July. If you really want to go out on a limb, how about a Halloween wedding, with the wedding party and guests coming in costume and with pumpkins for a centerpiece?

The All-Nighter

This is a wedding celebration that's planned to last through the entire night. In some cases, the group rents an additional hall after the first reception. In others, the festivities continue at a private home. The wedding usually comes to a close with breakfast the next morning. Coffee, anyone?

A Weekend Free-For-All

You've heard of an all-nighter, well this is an all-weekender. Usually, a weekend wedding is set up like a minivacation for you and your guests, and takes place at a resort or hotel.

The Honeymoon Wedding

Not everyone's cup of tea, but then again not as bad as it sounds. The honeymoon wedding is akin to a weekend wedding. Guests are invited to a romantic honeymoon-type locale such as a resort or an inn, where they can stay with the new couple for a few days. After the honeymoon wedding is over, the bride and groom depart for the real (and much more private) thing.

A Moveable Feast

Like to travel? In the progressive wedding variation, the bride and groom attend a number of wedding festivities carried on over a period of days—and located in different places! Depending upon your budget, your love of travel, and the availability of friends and relatives to celebrate, you might start with your ceremony on the Eastern Seaboard, have a reception in the Midwest, and wrap things up in California. (Not all progressive wedding celebrations are that far-flung; many stay in the same state, even the same city.)

"Surprise! You're a Wedding Guest!"

The surprise wedding is a surprise not to you (we hope), but to your guests. Invite people to a standard-issue party, and if those in the know can keep a secret, your guests will be completely surprised when they arrive at a wedding.

A Trip Down Memory Lane

Stroll down Memory Lane with your groom, family, and friends by having the wedding at a place of special significance to you as a couple. Perhaps you want to return to the college where you two met, or the park where he proposed.

A No-Frills Wedding:

After all these grand suggestions, it's easy to forget that sometimes the most beautiful and enjoyable weddings are the ones that are the simplest at heart. Without frills and thrills, the meaning of the marriage celebration becomes clearer, and you realize that no matter where you are, it is who you're with that is important.

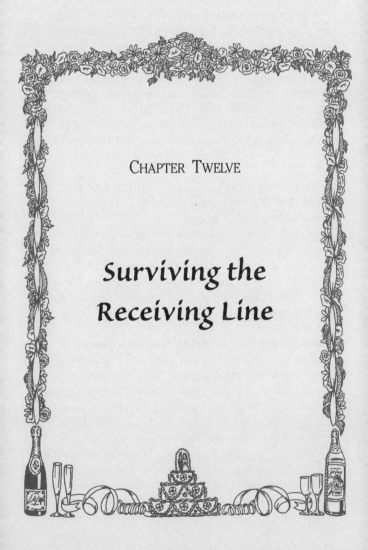

CHAPTER TWELVE

Surviving the
Receiving Line

The receiving line receives a fair amount of bad press these days, and it's usually the first tradition to get the ax. But it doesn't have to take up an agonizing chunk of time, and can be a lot of fun for you and your guests. The receiving line enables you, your groom, and key members of the wedding party to meet and greet your guests—which is very important, since you probably will not have time to socialize with everyone at the reception. Imagine painstakingly choosing the perfect gift and traveling for hours to attend a wedding, and not even having the opportunity to congratulate the bride and groom!

We're having a rather large wedding and are afraid that the receiving line will last forever. How can we speed it up?

If you're worried about the line taking up too much time on your big day, consider having a very fast, informal one at the back of the church or synagogue or outside the ceremony site. You greet your guests as they file out of the building. Then everyone can hop into their cars and speed off to the reception!

When should the receiving line take place?

The receiving line should form after the wedding ceremony but before the reception. If you and your groom are not immediately proceeding to the reception (because you're taking photos, for example), you should have the receiving line at the church or synagogue. Be sure to check with your officiant first; some have restrictions as to where the line may be formed. The most convenient spot is often near an exit or outside, where guests can move through easily on their way to the reception. If you choose to have the line at the reception site, have refreshments and entertainment available for guests while they're waiting.

Who stands in the line?

Although your bridesmaids traditionally join your families in the receiving line, this often makes for a slow and tedious process. Your best bet is to keep the receiving line small—your guests will thank you! The order from the head of the line is: bride's mother, bride's father, groom's mother, groom's father, bride, and groom. Your honor attendant may also join you on your left, but the best man does not usually join in the receiving line. It's optional for fathers to stand in line; they may prefer to mingle with their guests.

How can I incorporate my divorced parents and their new spouses in the receiving line?

The simplest solution is to have the fathers mingle with the guests rather than stand in line. If you would like to include your father (particularly if he's hosting the celebration), the order is: your mother, your groom's parents, you and your groom, and your stepmother and father.

What should I say?

You should welcome your guests, thank them for coming, and introduce them to the other members of the wedding party. If a guest is unknown to you, your groom or someone else in your wedding party may introduce you. Be friendly but brief—otherwise the line may become too long.

Neither I nor my fiancé want to include a receiving line. What else can we do to ensure that all our guests feel welcome?

Although there's no substitute for the receiving line where etiquette is concerned, you can still keep up appearances by making yourself available to your guests during the reception. If you choose not to have a receiving line, it is imperative that you make the rounds to greet your guests. The best time to do this is after the meal, when the dancing has started to heat up. You may want to hand out favors, such as decorative bags of mints, small candles wrapped in ribbons, or a cut flower (for women only), along with a few words of thanks to your guests for their attendance.

CHAPTER THIRTEEN

Better Keep 'Em Happy: The Seating Dilemma

rying to come up with a seating plan that pleases everyone isn't impossible, but it may very well seem so at times. It's best to realize early on that no matter how hard you try, someone—your mother, your fiancé's mother, your cousin Marta—is bound to be unhappy with some aspect of the seating plan. Don't lose any sleep worrying about who Aunt Sue should sit with. The easiest way to approach the seating plan is to get input from your mother and future mother-in-law; if possible, the three of you should sit down and come up with the plan together. If you all have equal input, coming up with a seating plan should go (relatively) smoothly.

Is a seating plan really necessary?

Unless you're planning a cocktail reception with hors d'oeuvres, a seating plan is a must. Guests, especially those who don't know many people, often feel uncomfortable without assigned seating. But if you're not planning to serve a full meal, you should have enough tables and chairs to accommodate all of your guests.

How can I let guests know where they'll be sitting?

The easiest way to alert guests to their table assignments is to place table cards at a table near the reception room entrance. Table cards simply list the name of the guest and their table assignment. Another option is to set up an enlarged seating diagram at the reception entrance. Simply posting a list of names and table numbers is not appropriate for a wedding reception.

Do I need to have place cards?

If you're planning a very formal wedding, place cards are necessary for all guests. At less formal receptions, place cards are used only at the head table. For everyone else, table cards are sufficient.

At the Head of the Class

The head table is wherever the bride and groom sit, and is, understandably, the focus of the reception. It usually faces the other tables, near the dance floor. The table is sometimes elevated, and decorations or flowers are usually low enough to allow guests a perfect view of you and your groom.

Who should sit at the head table?

Traditionally, the bride and groom, honor attendants, and bridesmaids and ushers sit at the head table. The bride and groom sit in the middle, with the best man next to the bride and the maid of honor next to the groom. The ushers and bridesmaids then sit on alternating sides of the bride and groom. Child attendants should sit at a regular table with their parents.

My mother believes that parents should sit at the head table with the bride and groom. I love my mother, but I only want the wedding party at the head table. Is my mother right?

Explain to your mother that the head table is usually reserved for the members of the wedding party; parents usually sit at separate tables with their families. There's no single correct seating arrangement for the parents, however. The bride's and groom's parents can sit together with the officiant and his or her spouse at the parents' table, or each set of parents can host their own table with family and friends. If your parents decide to include separate parents' tables, be sure that one of them includes the officiant and his or her spouse.

We're having a rather large wedding party. How should we handle the head table?

One large head table is usually fine for a large wedding. But if your reception site doesn't have tables big enough to accommodate your wedding party, you and your groom can sit alone at the head table. Or you could sit with your honor attendants at the head table and seat the rest of your attendants together at a smaller table.

Where should attendants' spouses sit?

They can sit at tables with the other guests. Spouses don't usually sit at the head table with their husbands or wives.

Not-So Musical Chairs

By this point, you have probably already realized that planning a wedding requires a little extra maneuvering if you have divorced parents. If you're lucky, either your parents get along or have agreed to declare a truce for a day. If you're not so lucky, seating arrangements can be a bit tricky. But as always, these problems can be solved through communication and flexibility.

My parents are divorced. What should we do about the parents' table?

You shouldn't seat your divorced parents at the same table, no matter how well they get along; people may get the wrong idea about their marital status. If you're having a parents' table, have the parent who raised you sit with your in-laws and the officiant, and seat your other parent with his or her own family and friends. Or, you can seat each parent at his or her own table with family and friends.

My fiancé's parents are divorced, and his father has remarried. It would be an understatement to say his mother and father don't get along. How should we handle this at the reception?

You should seat your fiancé's mother and father as far away from each other as possible in order to minimize interaction. However, don't seat one parent near the kitchen and the other near the head table; this might lead to even more friction. Try to seat both near the head table; this way, you have less of a chance of offending someone.

CHAPTER FOURTEEN

Right in Tune: Reception Music and Dancing

Reception music and entertainment can often determine the tone of the whole party. You may have planned a very elegant evening reception complete with free-flowing champagne and lobster Thermidor for dinner, but if the band starts playing Guns N' Roses covers during the cocktail hour, the romantic evening of which you've dreamed will most likely be soured a bit. You should be sure that your band or DJ can play a mix of music; you and your friends may be huge Madonna fans, but chances are your grandmother and mother-in-law are not. Different styles of music will keep everyone happy, and who knows, by the end of the evening, your mother may even join in the electric slide.

I've heard that you shouldn't have a DJ at a formal wedding. Is this true?

Traditionally, bands have been considered to be more formal than a DJ. But since bands are also considerably more expensive than DJs, either has become perfectly acceptable at a formal wedding.

I want to have a very elegant wedding, and I'm afraid a band or DJ will ruin that mood. Do I need to have entertainment?

It's possible to have music at a reception without forfeiting elegance; entertainment doesn't necessarily mean a loud band playing "Achy, Breaky Heart." You can always hire a string quartet or jazz ensemble to play at your reception. Or, hire a DJ or a piano player and ask him to play show tunes or standards by Billie Holiday or Frank Sinatra. Unless your religion strictly forbids it, you should try to have some form of entertainment. Not only do guests expect music and dancing, but many guests, especially those who don't know many people, may feel uncomfortable without entertainment.

May I Have This Dance?

The bride and groom's first dance is often one of the most romantic parts of your reception. You and your new husband, in what may well be your first and only appearance on a dance floor together, dance (or sway) to a song that the two of you have carefully chosen for its sentimental value, while your guests look on. Even the most hardened cynic can't help feeling nostalgic at the sight of a bride and groom dancing their first dance together as husband and wife.

Who dances after the bride and groom?

Traditionally, the bride dances with her father, and then the groom dances with his mother. Afterward, the bride's and groom's parents dance, the bride dances with her father in-law, the groom dances with his mother-in-law, and the bridesmaids and ushers dance with each other. Then open dancing begins. Of course, you may eliminate some or all of these dances if you choose, and simply have the band leader or master of ceremonies announce that open dancing will begin immediately.

We have more ushers than bridesmaids. How should we handle the wedding party dance?

You have a few options. You could either have a bridesmaid dance with two different ushers (not at the same time, of course), or just have some of your ushers sit out the wedding party dance. Chances are, they won't mind.

I'm close to both my father and stepfather. With whom should I dance the father-daughter dance?

This depends entirely upon your relationships with your natural father and stepfather. If your natural father is walking you down the aisle, he might not mind if you dance with your stepfather. Another option is to dance with your natural father, and have your stepfather cut in. Or if you're really in a quandary, dispense with the father-daughter dance altogether and just declare an open dance.

My family is Italian. Is it all right to incorporate ethnic music into our reception?

Definitely! Including music and dancing from your family's ethnic heritage is a wonderful way to spice up your reception. If you're Italian, have the band play a couple of Tarantellas; if you're Jewish, the hora is a fun, traditional folk dance that lights up the dance floor. If your guests have strong ethnic ties, they'll feel right at home, while guests of different cultures will enjoy learning something new.

CHAPTER·FIFTEEN

Here's to You: Wedding Toasts and Other Traditions

Wedding receptions are famous for their traditions. It's probably the only social event where guests actually know (or think they know) exactly what should happen when. Some traditions are virtually required—the first dance or bouquet toss, for instance. Others, like the dollar dance, are less common, and are found mainly within certain ethnic groups or regions of the country. Still, you shouldn't feel obligated to include a tradition in your reception if it's one you've never particularly cared for. Also, be careful if you want to try something new at your reception—your guests may feel uncomfortable if it's something they've never seen before.

What is the proper time for the best man to make the first toast?

After the receiving line has ended (finally!) and the wedding party and guests have been seated, everyone is served a glass of champagne or another sparkling beverage. The best man then stands up and toasts the newlyweds. The rest of the guests stand, too, but the bride and groom remain seated. Once the toasting is over, the dancing is started and dinner is served.

What is the toasting order at the reception?

After the best man, the groom can make a toast, then the bride, and then the parents, members of the wedding party, or other special guests can toast the newlyweds. After the toasting is completed, the best man can read any congratulatory telegrams that may have been received.

The order of the toasting can be:

- Best man toasts the bride
- Groom toasts the bride
- Bride toasts the groom
- Father of the bride toasts the couple
- Bride toasts her groom's parents
- Groom toasts his bride's parents
- Father of the groom toasts the bride
- Mother of the bride toasts the couple
- Mother of the groom toasts the couple
- Everyone else who has a wish to offer
- And so on, as long as the champagne and good-will hold out! (Note: All toasts except the best man's toast are strictly optional.)

What is the proper way to make a toast?

Like any other ritual, toasting has its etiquette. It helps to sort things out in the midst of merrymaking. Here's how it's done: To make a toast, stand up, tap on your glass to get the crowd's attention, and go to it—saying something like "Ladies and gentlemen, I have a toast to make," or "I have a few words to say." Meanwhile, the "toastee"—the person being toasted—does not drink at the end of the salute, but simply smiles at the toaster. Finally, a wedding toast shouldn't take longer than three minutes—more than that and it's overdone! The tone can range from serious and sentimental to humorous.

What kind of toasts are appropriate for the reception?

Reception toasts are usually a little more serious and sentimental than rehearsal dinner toasts. A toast from the best man could go something like, "To my best friend Jim, and his beautiful new wife Andrea. May we all experience the kind of love and happiness they share."

Let Them Eat Cake

The wedding cake originated in medieval times as a symbol of fertility. In ancient Rome, a loaf of wheat bread was broken over the bride's head to symbolize hope for a fertile and fulfilling life. The guests ate the crumbs, believed to be good luck. The custom found its way to England in the Middle Ages. Guests brought small cakes to a wedding; the cakes were put in a pile, over which the bride and groom later stood and kissed. Apparently, at one such shindig, someone came up with the brilliant idea of piling all the cakes together and frosting them, thereby creating an early ancestor of today's multitiered wedding cake. But before you decide to abandon the whole wedding cake idea, rest assured that for the most part the cake has since lost most of its symbolism and is now considered more of a deco- 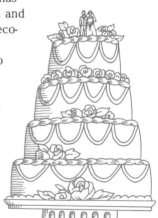 ration. Most wedding cakes are elaborately decorated and are so beautiful, you're almost afraid to cut into them. You and your groom usually cut the first piece together, and then feed each other a bite. The caterer or baker then cuts the rest of the cake and distributes it to guests. Some couples like to freeze the top tier of the cake so that they can eat it on their first anniversary.

When should we cut the cake?

At a sit-down reception, the cake is cut right before the dessert (if any) is served. If the reception is a buffet, the bride and groom cut the cake later in the reception, usually soon before they leave.

My fiancé's mother thinks we should have a groom's cake, but I've never heard of that. What is it and is it appropriate to have one?

Anyone who's seen *Steel Magnolias* is probably familiar with the groom's cake. It's usually a fruitcake or other dark cake, such as chocolate, which is cut and put into boxes as a favor for guests. Many grooms have a cake

 How to Cut the Wedding Cake

In case neither the baker nor the caterer is there to help you out, here's a quick guide, so you can cut your cake and eat it too.

- Cut vertically through the bottom layer to the edge of the second layer.
- Then cut wedge-shaped pieces.
- When these pieces have been served, do the same with the middle layer. Cut vertically around at the edge of the top layer.
- Then cut wedge-shaped pieces.
- When those pieces have been served, return to the bottom layer.
- Repeat the cuts made in steps 2 and 4.
- The remaining tiers may be cut into desired-size pieces. Bon appetit!

made in the shape of a favorite hobby, such as a football. Groom's cakes are very common in the South, but their popularity is growing in other regions as well. In the very old days, the groom's cake was referred to as the wedding cake, and what we now call the wedding cake was known as the bride's cake. Why the terminology was reversed is pretty much anyone's guess. However, as legend has it (who comes up with these things?), single guests who sleep with a piece of groom's cake under their pillow will dream of their future husband or wife.

Tossing the Garter and Bouquet

This most dignified custom began during the 1300s in France, where guests used to chase the bride and tear off her garter, ostensibly because they believed it was good luck. To save herself, her leg, and her dress, the bride began removing it voluntarily and tossing it into the eager crowd. Later, the bouquet was added to this toss. The lucky recipient of the bouquet is now believed to be the next woman in the group to get married. The man who catches the garter is supposed to be the next groom.

Here Comes the Next Bride

The tossing of the bride's bouquet is an example of how a tradition that was once widely accepted can gradually lose favor. Today, many brides find this tradition—in which the bride throws her bouquet to a group of single women, while the groom removes the garter from the bride's leg and then tosses it to a group of single men—to be degrading. As a result, many brides decide to eliminate this tradition in whole or in part, or find some fun alternatives.

Can you throw the bouquet without tossing the garter?

Of course! If you feel uncomfortable with the garter toss, as many brides do, it's perfectly acceptable to eliminate that tradition while keeping the bouquet toss.

I want to keep my bouquet. Would it be all right if I omitted this tradition?

You can observe the tradition of tossing the bouquet and still keep the one you walked down the aisle with. Many brides buy a separate bouquet to toss, or have the florist add a detachable, smaller bunch to their regular bouquet. When the time comes to toss the bouquet, simply pull out the smaller bunch.

There won't be many single women at my wedding. Do I need to toss the bouquet?

As with all wedding traditions, nothing is absolutely mandatory. If you feel your guests won't expect you to toss the bouquet, you don't have to. If most of your guests are married, here is a fun alternative that is gaining popularity: at the time you would normally toss the bouquet, invite your married guests to the dance floor for a special dance. Your band leader, DJ, or master of ceremonies then eliminates couples according to how long they've been married. The bride then awards the bouquet to the last couple on the floor (the couple who has been married the longest).

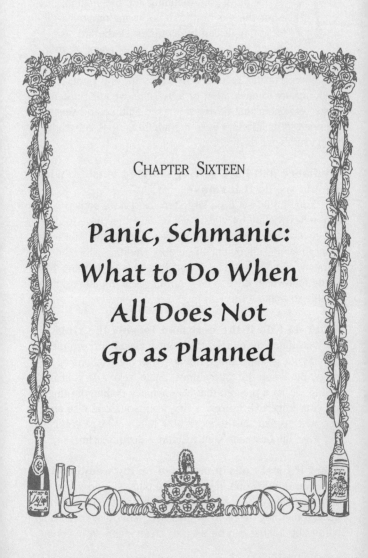

CHAPTER SIXTEEN

Panic, Schmanic: What to Do When All Does Not Go as Planned

Despite all of your planning and preparation, something is bound to go wrong on your wedding day. It can be as minor as the limousine being fifteen minutes late, or as major as your father and stepfather getting into a shouting match at your reception. For this reason, don't try to have a "perfect" wedding—try to have a fun or a beautiful wedding instead. Also, remember that having a relaxed attitude and sense of humor will ensure that even if something does go wrong, it won't ruin your day!

My fiancé and I are getting married outside. What should we do if it rains?

You should set up a large tent, and have some umbrellas waiting for guests just in case they have to run for cover. If you live in a rainy area, like Seattle, you may want to avoid scheduling an outdoor wedding altogether. Similarly, if your wedding is during the winter months, have some four-wheel drive vehicles available if the limousine is unable to make it through the snow and ice.

What do I do if the best man forgets the ring?

Assuming, of course, that your maid of honor remembered your groom's ring, continue with the exchanging of rings. But when the time comes, smile, relax, do your best acting job, and pretend that he's actually putting the ring on your finger. Or borrow a ring from someone else and use that instead. Just think of how much mileage you can get from his best man's little blunder down the line.

What if I stain or rip my gown on my wedding day?

You or someone in your bridal party should make sure that safety pins, a needle, and thread are close by in case something needs to be mended. Also, ask your bridal salon about what can be used to clean stains from your wedding gown; you can't simply throw club soda on the fabric of most wedding gowns.

What should I do if I have a problem with a vendor (DJ, caterer, photographer) the day of the wedding?

In most cases, mistakes like that can be avoided through careful planning. The easiest way to prevent disasters with wedding professionals is to get references from people who've worked with them in the past. Also, never pay for any services 100 percent in advance and make sure that your contract includes a clause that states that if goods are not delivered as stipulated in the contract, you will get a full refund of your deposit. To be safe, give a trusted friend a list of the names and phone numbers of all your vendors; he or she can call them if you experience any problems. This "what if" scenario is probably the best argument for hiring a wedding consultant; he or she will have years of experience in dealing with vendor problems, and if, by chance, something does go wrong, he or she can take care of it.

More Possible Problems

Unfortunately, not all possible problems are necessarily the result of poor planning or misguided wedding professionals. Some problems, especially those involving feuding families, cannot possibly be predicted. Of course, there is no single correct answer to any question regarding family difficulties. You and your fiancé must discuss with each other and your families what to do in case any family tensions flare up at your wedding or if an unexpected tragedy occurs before your wedding.

My brother is seriously ill. He wants us to go ahead with the wedding if he dies, but I don't think this is proper. What should I do?

You should carry on with the wedding in accordance with his wishes. A poem, song, or Scripture reading during the ceremony could honor his memory, as could a toast at the reception. Naturally, you should try to tone down the music at your reception; your guests will probably be in a more somber mood, anyway.

What can I do if my husband's ex-wife shows up at the church uninvited?

If you don't think she will make a scene or otherwise ruin your wedding, don't worry about it. But if you think she intends to cause an uproar, alert your ushers to this so that when she arrives, they can quietly ask her to leave.

I'm afraid that my divorced parents will make a scene at my wedding. How can I prevent this?

Speak with your parents openly and honestly about your concerns, requesting their cooperation and their best behavior. With any luck, they will be able to put their grievances aside for one day for your sake, but it's best to take precautions. Remind them of how much this day

means to you. To be safe, don't schedule any events that require divorced parents to interact. Seat them at separate tables, each with his or her own family and friends. Be sure also to let your wedding coordinator and other wedding professionals in on these family tensions. You don't want the photographer insisting on photographing the parents of the bride together if they can barely tolerate being in the same room.

Saying that my natural mother and my stepmother don't get along is a major understatement. How can I avoid any upsetting or embarrassing situations on the big day?

You should try to keep them apart as much as possible, seating them far away from each other during the ceremony and reception. If you have a wedding consultant, he or she can be a big help in trying to keep the peace within your family.

Let's Call the Whole Thing Off

In some cases, you may never even get to your wedding day—you and your fiancé may have decided you both would be better off if you didn't get married. Breaking an engagement is a difficult and painful decision, and figuring out what to do with the engagement and wedding presents you've already received is probably the last thing on your mind. Still, there are some guidelines that should be followed if you and your fiancé have canceled your wedding.

Should I keep my engagement ring or give it back to my fiancé?

Traditionally, the person who breaks off the engagement gives up the ring. Even so, if he initiated the break-up, you probably don't want it, anyway. If the decision was mutual,

then you should offer the ring
back to your ex-fiancé.
Obviously, if the ring was an
heirloom from your family, you
can keep it, regardless of who
broke off the engagement.

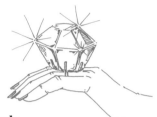

If our invitations have already been sent out, how should we notify guests?

If time permits, print cards that say "Mr. and Mrs. John
Lindsey/announce that the marriage of their
daughter/Caroline Jane/to/ Eric Stephen Martin/will not take
place." If there isn't enough time for this, you and your ex-
fiancé should phone your guests to tell them personally of
the cancellation. You should also send a short note to the
newspaper that carried the original announcement.

What should we do with the engagement or wedding gifts we've already received?

You should return all gifts to their senders along with
a note thanking them for their kindness but explaining that
the wedding will not take place. This includes all gifts that
have been monogrammed. If you received any checks or
cash, you should send the money back as well. And if you
jumped the gun a bit and already started using some of
your wedding gifts, buy replacements and send them back.
Under no circumstances should you send a used gift back
to the sender.

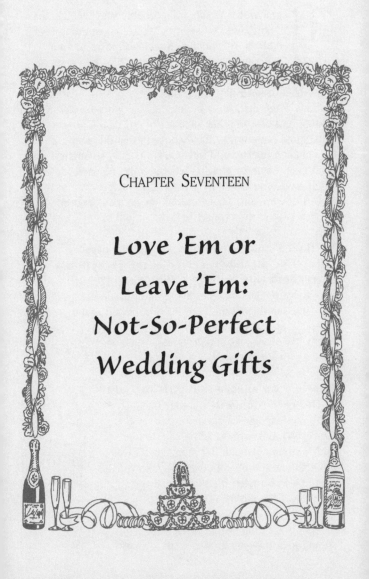

CHAPTER SEVENTEEN

Love 'Em or Leave 'Em: Not-So-Perfect Wedding Gifts

*Y*our wedding gifts will probably start trickling in soon after you send out your first wedding invitations. As you get closer and closer to your wedding date, this trickle can turn into a steady stream. This is fun for two reasons: first, you get to come home from a hard day at the office and open a beautiful package every day; second, you can see who decided to splurge and buy you that $300 set of cookware. On the flip side, some people may have chosen to ignore your carefully chosen registry and buy you something so strange you can't even begin to imagine what it could be used for. In either case, you would be wise to keep a very careful record of who sent what. After all, those thank-you notes are just around the corner!

My fiancé's mother thinks we should display the gifts we've already received at the reception. I don't think this is proper. Who's right?

You are! Gifts may be displayed at home before the wedding, but they should never be displayed at the reception site. Also, monetary gifts should never be displayed; checks should be deposited as soon as they're received.

How can we ensure that gifts brought to the reception will be safe?

Generally, guests should not bring gifts to the reception—they should be sent to the bride's home, instead. But many guests will bring gifts to the reception anyway, so you should ask a trusted friend or relative to watch over the gift table while guests are still arriving at the reception site. Once the reception is in full swing, he or she should lock the gifts in a special room. Also, if the reception is in a hotel, lock any money envelopes in the hotel's safe deposit box. The best man or other friend should check the gift table frequently and put any envelopes in the box right away. Check with the manager of the reception hall to see if such a room is available. If you're leaving for your honeymoon straight from the reception, have someone bring the gifts from the reception site to your home.

We've received duplicate wedding gifts. Can we exchange them?

Of course! But it's a good idea to wait until you've received most or all of your presents before you begin exchanging them; you don't want to exchange a toaster for a cappuccino maker only to get another cappuccino maker a week later. Also, unless your storage space is extremely limited, some duplicate gifts are worth keeping—you can always use a few extra glasses or another set of towels.

What if we've received gifts that we don't care for?

This is a very tricky issue. On one hand, what on earth are you going to do with a bronzed bust of John Lennon? On the other hand, how can you possibly get rid of it when the sender is your fiancé's favorite uncle who stops by once a month? In this case, the easiest solution would be to keep dear John in the back of a closet, and take him out whenever this uncle comes over. In cases where the sender is not such a frequent visitor, you can probably get away with returning the gift in question for something a little more in keeping with your taste.

What do we do if we receive damaged gifts?

If the gift came through the mail and was insured, let the person who sent it know so that he or she can collect the insurance money. If the gift was not insured or did not come through the mail, try to find the store where the gift was bought and exchange it; don't tell the sender that the gift was damaged. But if you're not sure what store the gift came from, try to discreetly find out from the sender where the gift was purchased.

If we haven't received a gift, should we mention it to a guest?

Even the strictest etiquette gurus say that guests have up to a year to send a wedding gift, so it would be inappropriate to mention it. But if you have reason to believe that the gift simply got lost in the mail, you may tactfully mention it.

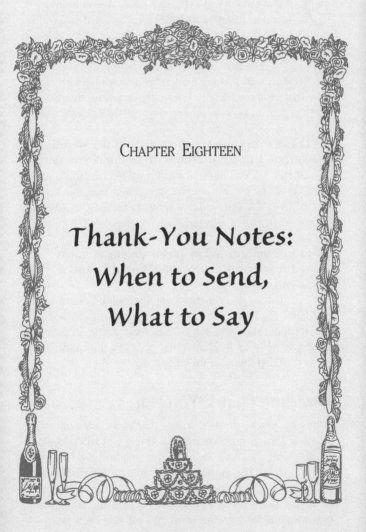

CHAPTER EIGHTEEN

Thank-You Notes: When to Send, What to Say

*I*t's a well-known fact that almost everyone hates writing thank-you notes. It's ironic that in today's world of instant communication, you are supposed to send a handwritten thank-you note every time you receive a gift. If you bump into someone on the street, you can't simply say, "Oh, Heather. Thanks for your gift. I can't wait to start making margaritas in that blender!" and have that be the end of it. For better or worse, thank-you notes appear to be one rule of etiquette that's here to stay.

If I thank everyone for their gifts at the wedding shower, do I need to send written thank-you notes?

Of course! You need to send a written thank-you note for every single gift you receive, regardless how much you gushed over it at the wedding shower. This also holds true for any engagement gifts you may have received.

My future mother-in-law threw an engagement party for me and my fiancé. Should I send a thank-you note?

Yes! During your engagement, you will no doubt have a number of parties thrown in your honor—engagement parties, wedding showers, and bachelorette parties. In each case, you need to send a written note to each of the hostesses thanking them for their generosity.

Wedding Thank-You Notes

Soon after you've finished writing thank-you notes for your wedding shower gifts, your first wedding gifts will probably begin trickling in. And naturally, this means more thank-you notes to write! The smart (and organized) bride will write a note the day she receives each gift; it's no fun to return from your honeymoon to find a hundred blank thank-you notes waiting for you. But since you will inevitably fall behind, at least send them out within three months after your wedding. Try not to write all of your thank-you notes at one sitting, though. Writing a hundred notes at one time will not only make your hand stiff, but they will start sounding formulaic and insincere.

What should I say?

You should make each thank-you note as personal as possible; try to name the gift and say how you and your fiancé will use it. A good example might be, "Thank you so much for the place setting of china. Dave and I are looking forward to throwing our first dinner party, and now we know the table will look great no matter how the food turns out! Thanks again for everything. We hope to see you again soon!" For odd gifts, try something like, "Thank you so much for the asparagus steamer. How did you know that Dave loves asparagus? I'm sure it's something we'll use often over the years. Thanks again for thinking of us!"

I heard that we have up to a year after the wedding to send a thank-you note. Can this be true?

Your incredulity is well warranted. The fact is that while wedding guests have up to a year to bestow a gift upon you and your spouse-to-be, you, dear bride, have only three months to come back with a thank-you note.

If I received a group gift, do I need to send thank-you notes to everyone?

No. If five coworkers chipped in to buy you one nice gift, five separate thank-you notes aren't necessary—just one, sent to your office, will suffice.

I've sent thank-you notes to everyone who got us a wedding gift, but I have a feeling that I should also send thanks to our officiant. Is this appropriate?

Certainly. Everyone who assisted in making your wedding day memorable should be honored with a thank-you note. That includes not only your officiant, but your wedding consultant, caterer, videographer, photographer, as well as any family members and friends that may have contributed their time, effort, and expertise.

Can we have thank-you cards preprinted?

No! Each thank-you note should have a handwritten, personalized message; preprinted notes rank right down there with writing where you're registered on wedding invitations.

Some people have sent their wedding gifts by UPS and Federal Express. Since the wedding isn't for another week, can I send the thank-you notes later?

_____This is not a good idea. The people who've sent their gifts via mail are likely to worry about the safe delivery of their parcels. Your prompt reply is the only way to allay their apprehensions, so don't delay—write those thank-you notes the very day of your gift's arrival.

If I write any thank-you notes before the wedding, should I use my maiden or married name?

You should sign your maiden name to any thank-you cards written before you're married. Don't start signing your married name until after your wedding.

More Thank-Yous

Additional examples of good thank-you letters can be found below:

Dear Ann and Billy,
    Thank you so much for the beautiful painting. We plan to hang it over the living-room fireplace for everyone to see. The colors really brighten up the room.

Fondly,
Ann

Dear Aunt Mary:
    Thank you for the lovely wine glasses; they really round out our bar set. Jim and I are looking forward to your next visit, when you can have a drink with us.

Warmest regards,
Ann

And that's all there is to it! See, thank-you letters don't have to be painful!

If we received a check instead of a gift, should we indicate the amount on the thank-you note?

No. You can write something like, "Thank you for your generous gift. It will come in handy when buying furniture for our new home."

Can my fiancé write thank-you notes?

Since wedding gifts are given to both of you, it is absolutely appropriate for your fiancé to do his fair share of the notewriting. What's more, his friends and relatives would most likely appreciate seeing a note from him personally. However, since only one person actually writes the note, you and your fiancé should sign only one name to the card; write "Love, Pam" or "Love, Tom," not "Love, Tom and Pam." Of course, whoever writes the note should always mention the thanks of their spouse/fiancé in the body of the letter.

CHAPTER NINETEEN

A Hassle-Free
Honeymoon

W hat with all the frenzied planning, coordinating, organizing, and worrying involved, getting yourself married can be a full-time job—and then some! When it's all over with, you'll need more than just an ordinary vacation to recuperate.

On the surface, a honeymoon is no different from any other vacation you might take. You pack your bags, make your reservations, and leave home for fun in the sun, snow, or whatever. But lets face it, to a pair of newlyweds, a honeymoon is much more than that; it's their first getaway together as a married couple, and perhaps the ultimate romantic experience. Ten years from now, you probably won't recall just when it was you spent that summer week in the mountains, or that long weekend skiing. But you're bound to remember nearly every detail about your honeymoon, wherever you may go.

My fiancé and I are at loggerheads. He likes to ski, I like to sunbathe. What should we do?

Arguing about where to take your honeymoon almost defeats the purpose. This is your time to gaze lovingly into each other's eyes, not spewing invective under your breath because you resent having been manipulated into vacationing at a ski lodge, or a beachfront resort. Before the situation escalates into a full blown deal breaker, take matters into your own hands and find a middle ground. How about Europe? As long as it's not the slopes of St. Moritz, Switzerland, both of you can have a good time taking in the sites, shopping, and savoring the fine cuisine.

Our families' finances are going to be kind of tight after the expense of the wedding. Can we put off the honeymoon until later?

Actually, more and more couples are foregoing the immediate honeymoon, opting instead for a quick getaway first and a honeymoon some months into the marriage. There's nothing other than tradition that says you must have your honeymoon right away. The bottom line is that the honeymoon is for you, and you alone, so you get to do whatever makes you happy.

For those in a similar situation who are dead set on honeymooning right after the wedding, consider traveling on a budget. With some research and planning, you can have a deluxe honeymoon on a shoestring. The honeymoon police won't arrest you for staying at a three-star hotel instead of that four-star number you had your eye on. Oftentimes, the less costly hotels come complete with loads more charm and quaintness than their pricey counterparts. Believe it or not (and you will once you've done your research), "inexpensive" does not mean "dilapidated," "roach-infested," "sunlightless" or "situated in the heart of the red-light district."

The Fine Art of Tipping

When, whom, and how much to tip are often embarrassing and confusing questions. In some situations you can ask your companions at the dining table in a hotel or on ship-board, or the management, but it's better to be prepared with some knowledge of the travel tipping structure.

We're going on a cruise. I've never been on a cruise before, what's the tipping etiquette?

Good question. Here's the answer:

Room steward: cleans your cabin, makes the bed, supplies towels, soap, ice, and room service. Tip: $3.50 per day per person. Tip at the end of the trip. Some also tip on the first day, "to ensure the perfect service"—a slogan said to be the origin of the word *tip*.

Dining room waiter and busboy: waiter, $3.50 per person per day, half that for the busboy.

Bartenders, wine steward, pool and deck attendants, etc.: check the bar bill. On almost all ships, a service charge is automatically added, making a tip unnecessary. Other service personnel should be tipped when the service is given, at the same rate as for service ashore, usually 15 percent.

Maitre d', headwaiter: in charge of the dining room. No tip is necessary unless he has handled special requests for you.

"No-tipping" ships: some cruise lines advertise a "no-tip" policy. People still tip for special services on such ships, but it is not necessary if you do not ask for anything "above and beyond."

What is the going rate for tipping at the airport?

You can't get away without tipping the porter $1 per bag when you check in at the curb or have bags taken to check in for you. Obviously, if you go the DIY route, no tip is necessary or expected.

I always feel as if I'm not tipping the hotel staff enough. What is considered standard?

Bellboy: $1 per bag, plus $1 for hospitable gestures—turning on lights, opening windows.
Tip on service.

Chambermaid: $1 for each service, minimum $5 per couple per week. Tip each day; a new chambermaid may be assigned during your stay.

Doorman: $1 per bag; $1 for hailing a taxi.
Tip on service.

Headwaiter: $5 per week for special service, $2–$3 for regular service—tip on your first day.

Wait staff: 15 to 20 percent of the bill when no service charge is added; some add 5 percent when there is a service charge. Tip at each meal.

Room Service: 15 to 20 percent of bill in addition to room service charge. If menu or bill explicitly states that a gratuity will automatically be added, you might add an additional $1 or refrain from tipping altogether.

Other service personnel: the general rule to follow is to tip 15 percent to 20 percent of the bill, unless the person serving you owns the business. Some owner-hairdressers, for example, do not accept tips, but charge more for their services.

Decisions, Decisions!

If you and your fiancé are having trouble settling on a destination, it might be a good idea to consider the most popular honeymoon spots. After all, the reservation agents won't wait forever; some of the most vied-after destinations may be booked up to a year in advance. Use the following lists to help you in your decision-making process and pick a place in no time.

In the Caribbean:
- Aruba
- Cayman Islands
- Little Dix Bay, British Virgin Islands
- Montego Bay, Jamaica
- Nassau, Bahamas
- Negril, Jamaica
- Ocho Rios, Jamaica
- Paradise Island, Bahamas
- St. Croix

In Mexico:
- Baja California region
- Cancun, Quintana Roo
- Guadalajara, Jalisco
- Isla de Cozumel, Quintana Roo
- Puerta Vallarta, Jalisco

In the South Pacific:
- The Marquesas
- Tahiti

In Europe:
- Greece
- Spain
- England
- France
- Italy
- Germany
- Austria
- Switzerland
- Sweden
- Finland
- Norway
- Monaco

In the United States:
- Alaska
- Hawaii
- Grand Canyon National Park, Arizona
- Niagara Falls, New York
- The California Pacific Coast Highway
- Hilton Head, South Carolina
- Poconos Mountains, Pennsylvania
- Disneyland, Anaheim, California
- Walt Disney World, Orlando, Florida
- Massachusetts Beach Resorts: Cape Cod, Martha's Vineyard, and Nantucket
- U.S. Virgin Islands

Note: Don't forget about more exotic locations like:

- Australia
- the Netherlands
- Japan
- South America
- Africa
- India

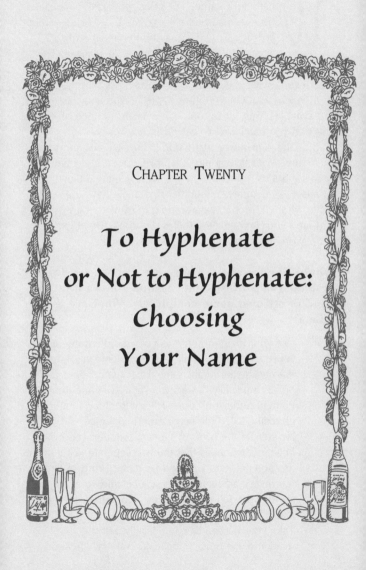

CHAPTER TWENTY

To Hyphenate
or Not to Hyphenate:
Choosing
Your Name

$\mathcal{W}$ hat's in a name? For years, you may have taken your own surname for granted. But faced with its possible loss, you may find yourself more attached to the name than you'd realized. This is the name you went through school with, the name you went to work with, the name everyone knows you by. It feels like a part of you. On the other hand, maybe your last name is 10 syllables long, or no one can ever pronounce or spell it right, and you can't wait to get rid of it.

If taking your husband's name is an easy decision, congratulations. Your task is much simpler than a lot of people's. For many brides, however, the decision is quite difficult. If you are in a quandary, remember that these days the only people who will probably care about it are you, your husband, and your immediate families. So don't spend lots of energy worrying about what everyone will think.

I would like to take my husband's name, but for personal and professional reasons, I don't want to abandon my own name completely. What are my options?

- Use your maiden name as your middle name and your husband's as your last. So if Jennifer Andrews married Richard Miller, she'd be Jennifer Andrews Miller. especially nowadays, when everyone from Pamela Anderson Lee to Hillary Rodham Clinton is choosing to go the way of the hyphenate.
- Hyphenate the two last names: Jennifer Andrews-Miller. This means that the two separate last names are now joined to make one name (kind of like a marriage). You keep your regular middle name, but saying your full name can be a mouthful: Jennifer Marie Andrews-Miller.
- Take your husband's name legally, but use your maiden name professionally. In everyday life and

social situations, you'd use your married name, but in the office, you'd use the same name you always had.

🜨 Hyphenate both your and your husband's last names: Jennifer Andrews-Miller and Richard Andrews-Miller.

How should I inform people of my decision to keep my maiden name?

Be sure to tell close family and friends about your decision first. Then, you may wish to tell all in one fell swoop by adding to your wedding announcement, "The bride will retain her name." Be sure also to tell the band leader or DJ at your reception how you would like to be introduced (for instance, "Jennifer Andrews and Richard Miller"). For a more personal touch, have both of your married names printed on your thank-you note stationery or combine them with your new address on an at-home card.

Besides family and friends, who needs to be notified of my name change?

If one or both of you will be changing your name after marriage, you should be sure to update the following:

🜨 Bank accounts
🜨 Car registrations
🜨 Credit cards
🜨 Driver's licenses
🜨 Employment records
🜨 Insurance policies
🜨 Internal Revenue Service records
🜨 Leases
🜨 Passports
🜨 Pension plan records
🜨 Post office listings
🜨 Property titles
🜨 School records or alumni listings
🜨 Social Security

> *Jennifer Andrews's name will be changed to Jennifer Miller as of May 27, 2000.*

- Stock certificates
- Utility and telephone information
- Voter registrations
- Wills

I have decided not to change my name after marriage. What do I do when someone incorrectly refers to me by my husband's name?

If this should happen to you, try to be patient. It's an assumption people commonly make unless they know otherwise. You can either let it pass, or politely correct the person, depending on how important the issue is to you. To avoid this awkwardness, you may wish to take the initiative and introduce yourself to strangers first: "Hi, I'm Jennifer Andrews, Richard Miller's wife."

I'm keeping my maiden name after marriage. I'm a little nervous about telling my in-laws for fear of offending them. How should I handle this?

You're right to be sensitive to your in-laws' concerns. Explain the reason for your decision (for example, that you've already established a career identity with your maiden name) and emphasize that your decision in no way reflects a lack of respect for their family. You may reassure them by saying that you plan to use your husband's name socially and/or that your children will take your husband's name, if that's the case. Ask your spouse to voice his support of your decision.

My fiancé and I are nearly coming to blows on the name issue. What should we do?

If you can't agree on any of the above solutions, and he almost fainted when you suggested that he adopt your surname, consider dropping both of your last names and finding a new one together. Otherwise, negotiation and compromise are the rule for the day. After all, that's what marriage is all about.

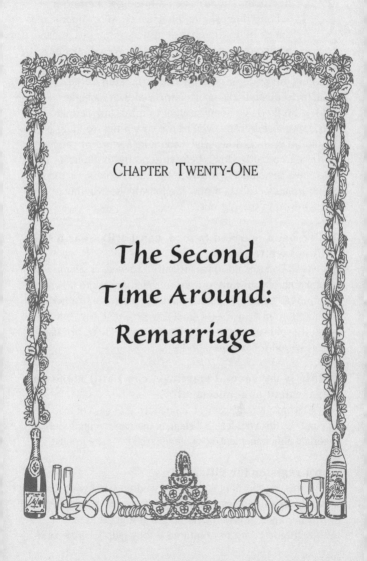

CHAPTER TWENTY-ONE

The Second
Time Around:
Remarriage

Once upon a time, when a bride got married a second time, she and her fiancé were supposed to sneak off to the nearest justice of the peace. No white gown, no guests, no gifts. Well, times have changed considerably. Now it's perfectly acceptable for a second-time bride or groom to have the kind of big, splashy wedding traditionally associated with first-time brides. So if you've been hesitant to make any definite wedding plans because you're not sure a big wedding would be proper, don't worry about it. A word of caution: If you had a big wedding before, don't try to duplicate it and have the same style gown, the same colors, or the same themes. This is a new life for you, so why invite comparison to the old one?

If I've been married before, can I still wear a traditional white gown?

Yes! You are no longer required to wear a simple pastel suit. If you want to wear a traditional white gown, go right ahead. White is not a symbol of purity, but rather of celebration and joy. You can still wear a veil, too, but you should avoid wearing a long, formal train. Those are usually reserved for first-time brides.

If this is my second marriage, can I still make an engagement announcement?

Customarily, engagement announcements are not made for any but the first wedding. Subsequent marriages require only a wedding announcement, so spare yourself the extra trouble.

Can I register for gifts?

If this is your fiancé's second wedding, but your first, yes, go ahead and register. But if this is your second trip down the aisle, registering is not such a good idea. Although guests are not required to buy gifts for a second-time bride, they may feel obligated to do so if you register. Some guests may want to buy you a gift anyway, so you might want to have a few items in mind just in case people ask.

Is it proper to have wedding showers or other prewedding parties?

If someone from your fiancé's side wants to throw a shower for you, fine. But don't expect anyone from your side of the family to throw you another shower, especially if you had a big one the first time around. Your friends and family should find other ways to celebrate your upcoming marriage, perhaps with a cocktail or dinner party. But you shouldn't have any type of function where guests are expected to bring gifts.

Can I ask my parents to help with the costs of another wedding?

In general, no, you shouldn't ask them to finance a second wedding, especially if they went into hock throwing you a lavish wedding 10 years ago. If you're a "mature" second-time bride, you and your fiancé should be able to finance your own wedding. But if your parents offer to pay for a second wedding, there's nothing wrong with taking them up on it.

Guest Lists for Second Marriages

If you or your fiancé have been married before in a big wedding, you know first-hand the problems that can arise in compiling a guest list. Hopefully you've learned how to deal with your stepparents and how to tell your future in-laws that they can't have twice as many guests as you without offering to pay for them. Because now, a whole new set of dilemmas await you.

Can we invite people to the wedding if they also came to my previous wedding?

Yes. Don't feel uncomfortable about asking friends to join you when you start your new life. Chances are, they've given you love and support through your divorce or widowhood. If it's gifts you're worried about, guests aren't under any obligation to buy you gifts for a second wedding.

My fiancé has a very young son from his previous marriage. Is it OK if he does not attend the wedding?

If the child is young enough that he won't remember the wedding anyway, letting him stay home may not be a problem. But if he's older, he should be there or else he may feel excluded from his father's new life. You can always ask one of his grandparents or another family member to look after him. Of course, check with your fiancé before making any arrangements for his son. It's also a nice gesture to have an older child serve as your honor attendant for your second marriage.

Should I invite my ex-spouse or ex-in-laws to the wedding?

Generally speaking, ex-spouses and ex-in-laws should not attend your wedding. But if you're exceptionally close with your ex-spouse (say the two of you got married when you were very young, and now you're good friends) then it's acceptable to invite them to the wedding. Of course, make sure your fiancé is comfortable with the idea before extending an invitation.

The Last Word

Etiquette is constantly evolving. What's considered standard practice today would have been considered shocking 20 years ago—and may seem old-fashioned in another 20 years. Most of today's wedding etiquette is fairly flexible, but there are still some etiquette "absolutes," like writing thank-yous when you receive gifts and not indicating where you're registered on wedding invitations. But if you skip over a chapter or two, and you do something "wrong," it's not the end of the world. There's no etiquette police to arrest you.

If you're unsure of how to handle a particular situation, or if you'd like to try something new at your wedding, but are not sure if it's proper, just use your best judgment. Common sense and good judgment are often the quickest and easiest answers to all your wedding dilemmas. Remember, it's your wedding, so have fun!

Index